Living on a Wing and a Prayer

MEMOIRS OF THE RAAF AND OUTBACK MINISTRY

Bob & Jenny Macintosh

Bob Macintosh

Writing this book on our memoirs has been an interesting time, as I do not see myself as a writer. But with the help I have received, it has been an enjoyable experience. The only thing I would like to add that is not mentioned in the book, is Bob's many talents. Not only was he regarded as a very good pilot in the RAAF, but he was also a very popular Commanding Officer of both 5 Squadron and the Base Squadron at Edinburgh, South Australia. More so, Bob was also a very good cake decorator, singer, ventriloquist, leadlight maker, and keen reader, especially science fiction. As well as building a garage and renovating a rumpus room, he was also excellent at fixing almost anything that broke. He even made himself a lap harp and taught himself how to play it. But most importantly he listened to other people with great understanding. To this day, many people still tell me how much they appreciated his gentleness and his help with their problems.

Jenny Macintosh, 2022

Living on a Wing and a Prayer

MEMOIRS OF THE RAAF AND OUTBACK MINISTRY

Bob & Jenny Macintosh

DoctorZed Publishing
www.doctorzed.com

Copyright © 2022 by Jenny Macintoshi

All rights reserved. No part of this book may be used or reproduced by any means, graphic, electronic, or mechanical, including photocopying, recording, taping or by any information storage retrieval system without the written permission of the publisher except in the case of brief quotations embodied in critical articles and reviews.

All the stories contained within are true, but some of the locations and people's names have been changed.

First print run 2022
Second print run 2023

First published 2022 by DoctorZed Publishing.
Revised first edition 2023

DoctorZed Publishing books may be ordered through booksellers or by contacting:

DoctorZed Publishing
10 Vista Ave
Skye, South Australia 5072
www.doctorzed.com
info@doctorzed.com

ISBN: 978-0-6455072-5-6 (hc)
ISBN: 978-0-6455072-6-3 (sc)
ISBN: 978-0-6455072-7-0 (e)

A CIP number for this book is available at the National Library of Australia. This is a work of non-fiction. The views expressed in this work are solely those of the author and do not necessarily reflect the views of the publisher, and the publisher hereby disclaims any responsibility for them.

DoctorZed Publishing first rev. date: 22/06/2022; second rev. date 22/02/2023

To Bob

A wonderful husband with many talents.

ACKNOWLEDGEMENTS

This book would not have finally come to fruition without help from my family, my great editor, Hari Teah, and all the assistance from Dr. Scott Zarcinas, DoctorZedPublishing.

CONTENTS

Chapter 1 – Growing Up: Bob
Chapter 2 – Growing Up: Jenny
Chapter 3 – Early Days: Bob
Chapter 4 – Courting: Jenny
Chapter 5 – The Korean War: Bob
Chapter 6 – Married Life: Jenny
Chapter 7 – Life in the RAAF: Bob
Chapter 8 – RAAF Family Life: Jenny
Chapter 9 – Malaysia & Vietnam: Bob
Chapter 10 – Malaysia, Vietnam & Australia: Jenny
Chapter 11 – Becoming a Patrol Minister: Bob
Chapter 12 – Outback Ministry: Jenny
Chapter 13 – Life in The Murchison: Jenny
Chapter 14 – The Annual Cricket Match: Bob
Chapter 15 – Women: Jenny
Chapter 16 – Children: Jenny
Chapter 17 – Animals: Jenny
Chapter 18 – Insects: Bob
Chapter 19 – Different Kinds of Shooting: Bob
Chapter 20 – Photography: Jenny
Chapter 21 – The Races: Jenny
Chapter 22 – Holidays: Jenny
Chapter 23 – Babtisms & Weddings: Jenny
Chapter 24 – Funerals: Bob
Chapter 25 – The Plane: Jenny
Chapter 26 – After Meekatharra: Jenny

Mavis Macintosh & Bob, 1929

CHAPTER 1

Growing Up: Bob

I was born on 12th March 1929 and am writing these recollections in Feb/Mar 2002. Most of what I will write is of hazy events seen from a particular point of view and often distorted by the mists of time. Nevertheless, they are written as honestly as is possible at this remove from the actual events! For these reasons, I have written it in the present historical tense and in the first person.

I Am Three Years Old
We live in the Shire Engineer's house at Rylstone. My little brother, Stuart, can't walk properly and can't talk at all! I know what he wants to say from the noises he makes. He takes up too much of Mummy's time. He is a pain! I am in the bath. My mother is on the telephone and ignoring my cries for attention. I decide to make so much noise that she can't hear on the telephone. This should bring her! The results are not to my liking. She doesn't come straight away. When she does come, she seems entirely unaffected by my efforts. I'll have to work out some other way!

I Am Four
I've got a proper tricycle! It's got spokes! Stuart has got my old Dinky tricycle with the solid wheels. My favourite book is a picture story version of *Robinson Crusoe*. I ask for it to be read every night and know the words almost off by heart. I have a

small friend who is three. I pretend to be able to read Robinson Crusoe to her. Just as I finish, I realise Mummy is watching. I *do* wish she wouldn't keep telling this story to all her friends! They always laugh.

An Adventure
I have found that if I take the tricycle to the top the hill, I can ride it all the way down the street with my feet off the pedals. Unfortunately, on the second run, the front wheel hits a pothole. The fork breaks and the front wheel comes off. I am covered in gravel rash. Daddy says he can get the fork fixed but it never looks as good again. Mummy says I can't ride it anywhere except in the back yard or the council yard next door. My cousin Tony has got a *real* bike! If I had a real bike, Stuart could have the tricycle!

A Lesson in Language
I overhear some of the council workers talking. I learn some new phrases. Mummy tells me to go and wash my hands.
    I say, "In your bum!"
    She washes my mouth out with soap. I won't use council men's language at home in future! Stuart still can't talk properly but we all know what he wants.

I'll Be Five in Two More Days
I'm down in the shed at the bottom of our large back yard. I'm climbing on the council grader and admiring the solid rubber tyres. Hidden behind the grader I see a bike! It's just exactly

like Tony's bike – exactly the right bike for me! I race home and tell Daddy.

"I'll tell you what," he says, "If you can ride it by your birthday, I'll give it to you for your birthday!"

I run down and wheel it out. I can't get on it. It keeps falling over. I take it up to the back verandah and get on and push off. It falls over. I do it again. And again. I keep on trying. I keep on falling off. After lunch I try again. Now I can go a few yards before I fall off. Quite suddenly it all comes right. I can ride it! It is the proudest moment of my whole life!

I'm Five and I Go To School
We learn the alphabet. I can read (sort of) but there are a lot of words that aren't spelled right. And a lot of others that are just too long. But now I really can read Robinson Crusoe – well, enough words to be a help, anyway. I'm terrible at colouring in and dancing but reading fascinates me and numbers are great. Kids don't like me much because I can't catch a ball and I'm good at reading. But I think I like school anyway.

On the way home from school a kid sets his dog on me. I face him for a while, but he runs in and tries to nip me. I run away. He bites a chunk out of my calf, but I keep running all the way home. Mummy bandages it up. Daddy says the health inspector will get the dog and destroy it. I'm pleased. Another day I see a dead dog on the way home from school. There are ants crawling in its mouth and flies all over it. That one won't bite anyone! I don't like dogs.

A Hard Lesson
We have got a car. It's an A model Ford, and it has a dicky seat at the back for Stuart and me. You can't see properly from the dicky seat, so Stuart and I like to stand on the seat and look through the back window. Daddy gets cross if he notices. We are going down a long hill. I stand up to see where we are going. The car hits a big bump and I fly out of the car and roll over and over down the hill. I pick myself up. The car keeps on going!

I run after it crying out, "Don't go without me!"

The car stops at the bottom of the hill and Daddy runs back to get me. I'm covered in gravel rash.

"Now do you understand why you must not stand up in the back?" says Daddy.

Mummy just hugs me. I never stand up in the back again. Stuart doesn't either!

I Learn To Swim
It is summer and very hot. Daddy and Mummy sometimes take us down to the Cudgegong River for a swim. It is only 200 yards from our house, across the common. There is a good place where kids can sit in the water up to their chests while the adults swim further out. The bottom is a gradual slope of sand. The water is muddy brown. I watch how the adults swim. I want to learn. I wonder if just pretending to crawl in the water would work. I try it in shallow water. It works! Another day we go to a farm and swim in the dam. There is a shallow area at one end for kids. The adults all swim in deep water but close enough to keep an eye on the kids. I 'swim' out to join them

– head up and 'crawling' as hard as I can go. I thought they would be pleased. They are not at all pleased. I am pulled back to the shallow end and told in no uncertain terms to stay there! Stuart pokes a face at me, but I don't care. I can swim!

Grandfather Comes To Stay

My grandfather's name is Andrew Macintosh. He is very old. His hair and beard are very grey. He sleeps a lot but when he is awake he sometimes plays with us. Stuart and I like him a lot. One morning I go into the room where he is sleeping and he wakes up.

"Come and play!" says I.

"I can't play today, I've got a bone in my leg!" says he.

"Poor grandfather!" I think. But as I go out I wonder if this is just an excuse, or maybe a joke or something. He seems all right later in the day anyway.

Stuart Learns To Talk

I am nearly six and I'm in first class. Stuart is in kindergarten. His teacher comes into our class and asks if I can come down to the kindy class to tell her what Stuart is saying. I'm embarrassed, but I go and tell her. This happens twice more on the first day. Stuart is mortified. He learns to talk much better in one day! By the week's end he talks as well as anyone else. If I ever have children, I'll make sure they can talk properly!

I Nearly Learn To Shoot

We go to a farm for the day. Mummy and Daddy play tennis and we watch. It's boring. The scores are funny. The have oil and juice and add in and add out. It makes no sense. I read my book to Stuart. He is not interested. We meet George. He is 12 and he has got a proper rifle. It fires .22 shorts. He uses it to shoot rabbits. He says he will show me how to shoot. We point the rifle at a tree and pull the trigger. It goes click. Then he puts a bullet in and shoots at a piece of paper on the trunk of the tree. George's daddy comes and says George can't shoot any more. But he says he will show Stuart and me how to shoot later. He doesn't. Daddy says he will buy me a rifle when I am twelve! (He doesn't).

We Move To The City
It is 1936. Daddy has got a new job. He is the Shire Engineer at Blacktown. We are going to have a house in the shire, but in the meantime we rent a house in Alice Street, Harris Park. There is a common at the back of the house and people ride their horses there. At one end of the street is a monument to Charles Rouse, who developed rust-resistant wheat and saved the colony. From the other end of the street you can see Elizabeth Farm, where John Macarthur lived. Stuart and I go to Rosehill Public School. Stuart is in first class and I am in second class. Mummy and Daddy tell us that Grandfather has died. Daddy arranges the funeral but we are not allowed to go. Funerals must be very scary—even Mummy doesn't go! I wish we could have seen more of our grandfather.

Not A Budding Rembrant
We are having an art lesson. Teacher says we have to draw a pencil picture of a dog. Afterwards she holds each of them up for us to see. Some of them are very good. Mine is the worst.

Everyone laughs. I will never be an artist, and anyway I don't like art!

A Birthday To Remember
Every Sunday we drive to visit someone. Aunty Meenie (real name Marian) and our cousins John and Tony live at Belmore. Nana and Heather and Valerie live at Chatswood. This Sunday we are visiting Nana because it is her birthday. I think she is 60. There is a big cake with a lot of candles on it and four people are using matches to light them. The flames join together and become a raging inferno. The icing is melting. Black smoke is rising. Heather takes a jug of water and pours it over the flames. The cake is taken away and returns later all cut into slices. It still tastes OK.

Moving Into Our Own House
After living in Harris Park for about nine months, we move into our new home in Northmead. Stuart and I share a bedroom. There is bush all around us and an orange orchard not far away. There is a big sandstone quarry about quarter of a mile away. It is full of water and birds swim around on it. Stuart and I try to hit the birds with stones but they are far too clever. We take an orange each from the orchard but they are too sour. We go to a new school – Northmead Public School. None of the kids wear shoes so we don't either. My teacher's name is Miss Scott. She is terrific! Life's good!

Boys And Girls
At our school there is a fence between the boys' playground and the girls' playground. The fence ends a few feet short of the school building. The only seating in the playgrounds is one long bench along the school building. The bench is always full, but there seems to be a strange rule that if you find yourself sitting next to a girl, both of you have to get up and walk away. The result is that there is always pushing so as to make that happen. It is a stupid rule, but at least there is constant movement and you can get a seat for a while.

One day after school, I join a game of 'keepings off'. I stub my toe on a rock and try hard not to cry. A little girl with great big blue eyes looks at me and says, "Gee you're brave!"

It makes me feel good. I'm brave. I'll never ever ever cry again.

Third Class
It is 1937 and I'm in third class, and Miss Scott is our teacher again! We recite our tables and I know them all. I am good at sums, even multiplication and division. One day the headmaster comes into our class and asks Miss Scott if any of her students can do division by twelve.

She says, "Bob can." Mr Deed takes me to 6th class and I do a division on the board for him. He thanks me and turns on the class.

"See!" he says, "Even a kid from third class can do it!"

Bob Macintosh, 13 Years Old

After school some big kids beat me up for showing them up in class. Still, Mummy is pleased with me and tells Daddy after he gets home. Daddy gives me two shillings and says he will give me five shillings if I come top of the class.

"What about me?" says Stuart.

I don't think either of us ever got paid.

A Loss Of Innocence
It is Christmas 1938. I am nine and Stuart is eight. We have a new brother. His name is Andrew, but we haven't seen him yet. Mummy and Andrew will spend Christmas in hospital and come home a few days later. Daddy tells us there is no such thing as Santa Claus and then takes us Christmas shopping. It is fantastic fun and I feel very grown up. I think I knew Santa wasn't real, but thought the presents would stop if I said anything. Anyway, it is a great Christmas. After Christmas, Daddy tells Stuart and me that we are too old to call our parents Daddy and Mummy. He says that we have a choice: either Mum and Dad or Mother and Father. Stuart and I go off to talk about it. We don't know anyone who calls their parents Mother and Father. That must be REALLY grown up. We decide to do it. Father seems pleased.

High School Days
In 1940 Father arranged for me to sit for scholarships to Sydney Grammar School and The King's School, Parramatta. I was successful, and in 1941 I started at King's. The uniform was based on the NSW Corps, circa 1870, and consisted of black trousers with red stripe down the seam, a salt and pepper tweed jacket with red cuffs and red epaulets, silver buttons, the school badge on red patches on the collar of the jackets, and school socks and black boots. As it was wartime my uniform was second-hand. We wore a slouch hat with a red puggaree and silver badge to complete the gear.

Back then, we only had three school terms. There were long holidays over Christmas – about six weeks – and short holidays of two or three weeks in May and September. There were school activities during the holidays, such as rowing training, Cadet Corps, NCO courses, and the like.

I was a day boy; supposedly an inferior class to the boarders, but I did well academically without really trying. In fact, I was put on the black list for three months to make me work harder, even though I was always at or near the top in tests. Even so, I was always a lazy student. Sport was very much the thing at King's, but unfortunately I was never really any good at it. I was 12 before I could reliably catch a ball, and my brother Stuart always beat me at tennis. I made the second four in rowing and the third fifteen in rugby union. My only school colour for sport was in shooting.

Physical fitness was promoted at King's. We had PT on Tuesdays and Thursdays, and 'round the park'—which was a run of about three kilometres—on Wednesdays. After any physical activity we always had a shower. Unfortunately, there was only one tap for the shower – the cold tap! It wasn't too bad in the warmer months, but in the winter term it was a pain. I think it was supposed to be healthy, but cold showers never became a habit.

I rode my bike to school for a number of years. It was about four kilometres each way on the Windsor Road. Traffic was fairly light due to wartime petrol rationing, but the hills were a trial as my load of books became heavier and heavier. Eventually I gave in, and caught the bus for my last two years at school.

We had dancing classes with a lady called Edna Williams. We took it in turns to be the girl. She insisted that we hold the 'girl' firmly, but it was not very well obeyed. About twice a year we had real girls in class from our sister school, Meriden. On these occasions, holding the girl tightly was even more difficult. If you don't know why, you are obviously a girl! I never much enjoyed dancing, except the bit about holding the girl. Nevertheless, dances were great places to meet girls, so I went to dances now and then. I don't have an opinion about the merits of single-sex schools versus co-education as far as academic results are concerned, but girls in class probably would have been a huge distraction for me!

In those days, the school was in Parramatta, on the bank of the Parramatta River. Parramatta is an Aboriginal word meaning, 'place where the eels reside'. Some of the eels were very big. One of the kids hooked a big one at lunchtime one day and it pulled so hard that he skidded and was pulled into the river. He had to be persuaded to let the eel go! Then he had to try to wring out his uniform because he was due back in class in a few minutes. He was not in my class so I can't say how the teacher reacted. A few days later he landed another big one, but it was so fierce he soon released it. It was about twenty centimetres wide and nearly two metres long, with lots of wicked looking sharp teeth. Truly, it was a fearsome monster!

We had a twenty-five yard swimming pool, and it was very popular in first and third terms. We swam at lunchtime and after school. We often came to school for sport on Saturdays so we could have another swim then. I was able to lie on the bottom with a lung full of air, and with all that practice I became quite a fast swimmer over short distances.

I made a number of really good friends at King's, but unfortunately I have lost contact with most of them over the years, as I lived far from Sydney after joining the RAAF, and then eventually retired to Adelaide: but I am getting ahead of myself.

I did reasonably well in the Leaving Certificate – well enough to go to university to study engineering. I was only 17, and very immature. The University of Sydney was filling with ex-servicemen who were able to balance a fairly wild social life with study. I fell by the wayside, but did learn how to play poker, solo, and other gambling games. I also experimented with alcoholic beverages and tried to like the taste of beer. I failed second-year engineering and had to look for a job.

The Interregnum
After leaving school I didn't really know what I wanted to do. I dabbled in politics. Labor was in power. I was elected President of the Parramatta Liberal Youth Club, which mainly comprised friends from school and some of the girls we knew. We sponsored a candidate to take on Eddie Ward in East Sydney. Of course, our candidate did not poll well, but we learned a lot about the political process.

After I left university I got a job as a stock clerk at William Adams. I worked in the office at Alexandria, which dealt with steel and other metal products. I kept records of stock in pounds, quarters, hundredweights, and tons. There are twenty-eight pounds in a quarter, four quarters in a hundredweight, and twenty hundredweights to the ton. So a ton is 2,240 pounds. Sometimes, I also had to work out the cost to the customer. Steel was sold by the ton – let's say the cost was £2/4s/6d. We had no calculator, just a book with complicated tables. Usually, it was quicker to just do the sums with a pencil and paper. When decimal currency and metric weights and measures were introduced in 1964 they would have been a great boon to my successor!

In 1949, along with three of my friends, I became part-owner of a 1929 model Oakland, which had been converted from a sedan to a utility. We had a ration of two gallons of petrol per month, but found that it would run on kerosene, which was not rationed, if you warmed up with petrol. We also ran it on mineral turps one occasion. Petrol rationing ended in February 1950, much to our relief.

We learned a lot about cars and their workings while we had the old Oakland. Probably the biggest learning experience was when we decided to replace the piston rings. We took some girls on a picnic and, while the girls dealt with the food we drained the sump, removed it, and dropped the pistons out. Then we replaced the rings, reassembled the bits, and refilled the engine with new oil we had brought with us. This all took about an hour and a half and we were filthy when we sat down to eat. The girls were *not* impressed! But the car ran very well and did not smoke, so we did quite well. I am assured that you could not change the rings in a modern car in an hour and a half, because modern cars have a shorter stroke and you can't get the pistons out from the bottom. You have to pull the whole engine apart. Another time, the fuel pump failed while we were driving. We siphoned petrol out of the tank into an empty lemonade bottle and raised the engine cover on the right side to expose the carburettor. Then we removed the air filter and I lay on the mudguard, pouring petrol directly into the carburettor while the car was driven to the nearest garage, where the membrane in the petrol pump was replaced by the mechanic before we drove on. As I said, we learned a lot about cars.

I left home in 1949 and went to live in a boarding house in Strathfield. I learned to darn my socks and do the washing and ironing – useful skills for any bachelor. I also decided that I would knit myself a jumper in diamond pattern. I already knew how to knit, having knitted a scarf for my father during the war. However, I knitted very tightly and girls watching me knit would offer to do a few rows. The first row they did took ages as my tight knitting made things difficult, but then they would do a row or two more before handing it back. I used to knit in the train on the way to work and drew a few stares from time to time. It took more than two years to finish, but it lasted for many years and always looked smart.

There was a beer shortage in 1950, and my father decided to join the ranks of the amateur beer makers. Having watched his efforts I persuaded my friends to make some of our own. We had the use of a ten-gallon stainless steel vessel from Rod Ward's father, who was a photographer by trade. The brew was very successful and was much appreciated by our friends. We took some of the beer to Sussex Inlet and camped by the inlet in great style. The fishing was sensational!

Rod and I decided to give golf a go. He borrowed his father's clubs and I borrowed my mother's clubs. They were very old with wooden shafts and cast iron heads, except the wood—which was entirely made of wood. They were a bit short for me, as my mother was only five foot three inches!

We drove in Rod's father's car to a nine-hole public course in Bankstown and sat watching for a while before we set off. Needless to say we had lots of problems, including an air swing or two, but we kept going until we were on the fifth green. As I lined up the putt, a Tiger Moth flew just overhead. The pilot had a big grin on his face. "He's having a lot more fun than we are," said Rod. So we walked back to the car and drove to Bankstown aerodrome, where we signed up for flying lessons at the Kingsford Smith Flying Club. Flying was quite expensive – £3/5s/0d per hour dual and £2/5s/0d per hour solo. I was earning £12 a week and paying £6 a week for board. What with fares, food, and social life (girls), I did not have a lot to spend on flying. Even so, I managed to pay for thirty hours in two years.

CHAPTER 2

Growing Up: Jenny

Learning To Swim

I don't remember learning to swim, but I do remember my only grandparent, my mother's father, taking me to the beach most days from a very early age. I was nearly six years old when my father was transferred from Melbourne to Wangaratta in northeastern Victoria, not long after the outbreak of the Second World War. One day we visited a relative with a pool, and was shocked to find that the water wasn't salty!

1. Iris & Kenneth Cleveland with Jenny
2. Grandfather Robert Kennedy with Jenny

Life In Country Victoria
As my father was away from Monday to Friday, and the family Chevrolet went with him, I had to walk the three miles to school every day, come rain or shine. I enjoyed living in the country. We had a lovely old home on 11 acres of land, much of which was pastureland for cattle. There was a creek near the house, which sometimes dried up to pools in the hot summers when the temperatures would climb up to the low 40s, only to replenish and run freely through the winter, except for the year when it froze over completely. There was a bridge over the creek, with a long drop onto rocks, but my favourite creek crossing was an old fallen tree.

We had a very big vegetable garden with a two lovely trees—a mulberry and a walnut. We also had numerous hens and a few roosters, some Muscovy ducks, and several turkeys. The latter were not my favourite, as I was often sent out with a tin of wheat to feed the chooks, and the turkey gobbler quickly learned that if he flew at me I would drop the tin. It became a battle for me to reach the chooks before he found me. One day we were having turkey for dinner and my mother told me that it was the gobbler. I enjoyed every mouthful even more. The ducks were my favourite, as they would often walk with me part of the quarter of a mile to our gate when I went to school, and meet me on the way back.

Learning To Cook
From about seven years old my mother taught me to cook on the wood stove, and by the time I was eight or nine I could cook a roast dinner, with a little supervision. The only way to

know that the oven was the correct temperature was to put your hand inside and do a Goldilocks test to see if it was too cold, too hot, or just right.

I Joined The Brownies
I would stay late after school one day a week to take part in the activities, which I enjoyed. Living as far out as we did there were no other children around to play with, so that made Brownies day special.

Family Life
We had a cellar, where I helped my mother make soap, which was not always easy to buy during the war, and where we could store butter and milk, as we did not have a refrigerator. We did have a Coolgardie safe in the kitchen, which was a metal framework with a container to hold water on top and a container at the bottom, which was covered in hessian. When the top was filled with water, and strips of towel were hung down the sides, it cooled the container at the bottom, so that small quantities of butter, milk, meat, and anything else needed for immediate use could be kept cool without the need to go down to the cellar.

One Christmas during the war, my sister was coming home on leave from the Air Force. Our father was picking her up on Christmas Day, and we were expecting them to arrive back at the house just before lunch. My mother and I had cleaned the house thoroughly and we were getting everything ready for Christmas lunch when we looked out of the window and saw a huge cloud of red dust approaching. There was a rush to make sure all the windows and doors were shut and to put towels across the windows before the dust storm arrived. After the dust storm passed it was a job to clean the house all over again, and then get on with food preparations. In those days the dust storms were a fairly frequent occurrence, coming over from the Mallee.

Back To Melbourne
In early 1945 we headed back to Melbourne and moved into a shared house, as accommodation was very hard to find at that time. I started going to school at Lauriston, but within the year I had caught rheumatic fever. After it was over the doctor would not let me go back to Lauriston, as they did not have heated classrooms, so I transferred to St Catherine's. As I'd had no children my age to play with for most of the time we were living in the country I was not very good with my own age group. The nuns at Wangaratta would point out to the class that I was not a Catholic, which left me struggling to fit in even more, although I still enjoyed school. I still have some good friends from my time at school in Melbourne.

Meeting Bob
When I was 16 I went to Sydney for the Christmas holidays, to stay with my aunt and uncle and their two boys. My mother's brother had married my father's sister, so the boys were double cousins. Angus was only three-years older than me, and Stuart was five-years older. It was during this visit that I met Bob Macintosh, Stuart's best friend. Although I stayed for most of the holidays, neither of us took a lot of notice of each other.

In fact, at the New Year's Eve party, I recall thinking that if Stuart's silly friend sang *Goodnight Irene* one more time I would throw something at him. Fortunately, he stopped before it got to that stage. A few days later, my aunt was driving us to cricket when Bob, drawing on all the wisdom of his twenty-one years, remarked on how annoying sixteen-year old girls were, with their incessant giggling.

CHAPTER 3
Early Days: Bob

Early Days In The Air Force

In 1951 I saw an ad in the paper calling for recruits to join pilot training in the RAAF. I jumped at it! I passed the medicals and finally arrived at Point Cook on 1st October 1951, to join No. 8 Pilots Course. It was then, and probably still is, the largest pilots course since the War.

On the first day we were issued clothing and marched to our barracks area, where we were met by Corporal Cowden. He told us where to go, which room was ours, where the showers were and so on. Then he showed us the parade ground and said, "Youse are to be here dressed in overalls at eight am tomorrer."

At eight o' clock the next morning I had just arrived at the parade ground. In fact, I was the last to arrive by the designated time. The stragglers were put in a group and told off in colourful language. The corporal explained that it was Air Force custom always to arrive five minutes early. Then he said we were to report to the parade ground every day at a quarter to eight.

"What time will you be here tomorrow?" he asked.

There was a chorus of, "A quarter to eight, corporal."

"WRONG!" screamed the corporal. "You!" pointing to one of the latecomers, "What time will you be here tomorrow?"

"Twenty to eight, corporal!"

"Right!" he said. "And anyone who's late will be on guard duty."

Punctuality is thus inculcated from the earliest days in the Air Force, and it becomes second nature very quickly. I am still pathologically punctual to this day.

On my first weekend leave, I decided to visit the only person I knew in Melbourne – Jenny Cleveland. I had first met her when she was visiting her Sydney cousins, who were friends of mine at school. She was then sixteen and I was twenty-one. Now, a year or so later, I turned up at her front door. She recognised me but couldn't even remember my surname. Nevertheless, I was attracted, and I visited her as often as I could over the next year and a bit.

Bob and Jenny, 1953

Our three months initial training included a bit of Air Force law, some aerodynamics, the rules of the air, the rules about saluting, lots of drill and, eventually, air experience – a few hours in a Tiger Moth. Those who passed everything except the air experience were offered navigation training, and several of our number accepted this path. Unfortunately, 'Their Airships' decided to add another twenty-five trainee pilots to our course, and sent us to Archerfield (near Brisbane) to do initial training all over again. Then we went to Uranquinty, near Wagga Wagga, in New South Wales, where we did basic flying such as aerobatics (loops, barrel rolls and so on), navigation, night flying, more on the Tiger Moth, and about 30 hours in the Wirraway. Finally, we were back at Point Cook for the advanced training on the Wirraway. This included some air to ground gunnery and dive bombing, as well as formation flying and more advanced navigation exercises. On the 12th December 1952, the thirty-seven survivors of the process received our wings and promotion to the rank of sergeant. I was posted to No. 2 Operational Training Unit at Williamtown, New South Wales, to train as a fighter pilot.

The course only took three months. We converted to Mustangs in the first week. Since there was no dual-control Mustang we just did some lectures, sat in the cockpit to learn where everything was, and then flew solo. Within days we were doing formation and dive bombing. We learned some of the skills of dog fighting and shot live ammunition at a target towed by one of the staff pilots. Then we concentrated on ground attack, including rocketry and air to ground gunnery.

Bob in Flying Gear

After this, we converted to the Vampire 30, a single-seat jet. In 1952 there was no dual-control Vampire and so, once again, we simply learned what we could about the aircraft and jet engines from books and spoken word, and then learnt by doing. The Vampire 30 was developed from a 1945 British design, but the RAAF decided to put in a larger engine – the Rolls Royce Nene. This necessitated the addition of two extra air intakes mounted on the upper fuselage, which had an unfortunate side effect. At about Mach 0.8 (80% of the speed of sound) a shock wave developed on the intakes and blanketed the tailplane, with the result that the nose went down and things got worse. Two pilots died before the fix was found. If this happened to you, all you had to do was close the throttle, extend your dive brakes, and wait a few seconds until the speed reduced below Mach 0.8 and everything returned to normal. Every pilot of Vampires had to do a 'Mach run' to experience the nose-down effect and to use the fix. It was quite a delightful aircraft to fly, and quite a pretty aircraft to look at. However, it had no ejection seat, and bailing out would have been quite difficult because of the twin tail. We were told that to bail out we had to fly upside down and trim full forward, which was supposed to throw you out far enough to miss the tail. As far as I know, nobody actually tried it.

After graduating from the Operational Training School I was posted to No. 77 Squadron to go to the Korean War. But first, we were given a few weeks of pre-embarkation leave. I went to Melbourne and proposed to Jenny. She accepted, but in those days parental permission was needed even for an engagement if either party was under twenty-one. Her mother said we would have to wait until her father came home before I could seek his permission. He worked in the country and only came home for weekends. I am sure Jenny's mother was convinced that her father would refuse, but in the event he was delighted to give permission. A party had been organised to farewell me and another member of 8 Course before we left for Korea. I asked for permission to ring my parents to announce the engagement. They lived in Coolah, a small New

South Wales town, and it was a trunk call. I dialled 011 and asked for Coolah 26. The girl on the switch said, "Yes sir, that will be about two hours."

"Oh dear!" I said, and explained we were about to start a party and I wanted to tell my parents I was engaged before announcing it at the party.

"Just a minute." she said, and connected me immediately! Apparently my plight was equivalent to a national emergency!

We had time to visit my parents so they could get to know Jenny before my posting to the war became active. One highlight was a visit to an amazing fossil site near Coolah, where I took this photo of Jenny. It captures the mood of the day perfectly.

They were great days, but all too soon I was off to the Korean War.

Jenny at the Fossil Site, 1953

CHAPTER 4
Courting: Jenny

Engaged

One Saturday morning in the October following my visit to Sydney, there was a knock at the door of our house in Melbourne, and there was Bob. He had joined the RAAF and was based in Melbourne. As he didn't know any people in Victoria he spent many weekends with us over the next 14 months. One thing led to another, and by December 1952 things were serious.

Bob returned home to Coolah that Christmas, knowing he would soon be going to Japan and then Korea to fly as a fighter pilot in the Korean War. Before leaving, he came back to Melbourne for a few days in February 1953, and proposed to me on a Wednesday afternoon. I was eighteen at the time and the legal age for becoming an adult was twenty-one, so although I accepted his proposal, Bob still needed to ask Dad's permission. As Dad was away until the Friday we went into town and chose an engagement ring on the Thursday. When Friday rolled around, Dad took Bob off for a quiet man-to-man chat, handing him a Scotch and waiting for Bob to get his nerve up. Even with the Dutch courage, Bob couldn't find the words until Dad prompted him by saying, "I believe you have something to ask me, Bob."

Once he'd asked permission for my hand in marriage, Dad readily agreed. Bob asked if he could ring his parents in Coolah to share the good news, and after an affirmative answer he went to ring the exchange, only to be told it would take two hours for the call to be put through. When Bob explained that he wanted to tell his parents the news of his engagement, the operator put him straight through. They must have cut some people off in order to do this.

Engaged, 1953

Although I was interested in going to university there was no point in starting a course if we were going to get married before I could complete my studies, as in those days you could not change which university you were studying at once a course had started, and with no internet there were no online courses.

So I decided to work until Bob returned from Korea, and got a job in a bank until he returned in March 1954. I worked in an office of about 40 people, and not one of them knew there was as Korean confrontation on, despite the fact it was in its third year. They very quickly did know. On the 27th July 1953 when the ceasefire was signed, one of the five men in the office brought in a transistor radio, something in 1953 none of us had seen. Very large by today's standard. Everyone in the office stopped for five minutes and listened to the signing of the end of fighting. Of course, this was great news for me as my fiancee would be coming home. For all of us in the office, it was the first time listening to something as it happened overseas.

We were married on the 27th April 1954. My mother suggested that I wore my maternal grandmother's wedding dress for the ceremony. At first, I was not convinced, as the dress was satin, and I thought it would not be suitable as I am so short. However, the dress was beautiful, a magnolia colour, very soft, with a bustle and train, large pleats on the skirt, and lace on the bodice. The dress is now held in Ayers House Museum in Adelaide.

The Wedding Dress

CHAPTER 5

The Korean War: Bob

After three months training at No. 2 Operational Training Unit (2OTU) I was posted to No. 77 Squadron in South Korea. Several No. 8 Course pilots, including myself, Frank Daniels, and Bill Monaghan, went on the same day. We travelled via Darwin to Iwakuni, Japan, in a Qantas DC4, with an overnight stop in Manilla. I was sent to No. 77 Squadron Training Flight to convert to Meteors. The Meteor was a twin-jet fighter, which first flew in 1944. The Meteor Mk8 was not up to mixing with the MIG 15, which was a swept-wing fighter with a copy of the Rolls Royce Nene engine. It could cruise at 50,000 feet and was capable of supersonic flight in a dive. The Meteor was limited to 40,000 feet and was much slower. For this reason, the Meteor was used as a ground attack aircraft and our training reflected this. Actually, the Meteor could give a good account of itself in a dog-fight with an MIG at lower altitudes, which is why we usually cruised at 16,000 feet on the way to the target and back. But I'm getting ahead of myself again.

We had some spare time in Iwakuni, and I found a beautiful Noritake dinner service which I purchased and sent back to Jenny in Australia. The shops in Iwakuni had lots of stuff aimed at the US and Australian service men who trained in the area. Prices were very reasonable, and packaging for export was done very well. We were there for the Cherry Blossom Festival, and enjoyed sampling sake and ogling the people in national dress. I took a great picture of a tiny Japanese girl in elaborate kimono and sash. She looked adorable.

The most important thing we had to learn was to fly on one engine if the other one failed. The Meteor had only one vice—it was hard to control if you had to abort a landing with one engine. Several pilots have been killed attempting it. You could not use full power on the remaining engine below about 190 knots, and it would climb only very slowly even at that speed. If you used full power at too low a speed the aircraft would roll over and head for the ground. We practised a lot, but fortunately I never had to do it in a real situation.

I arrived at K14, the 77 Squadron Base, in Kimpo, Korea, in late April, and was almost immediately sent off in a formation of 16 aircraft to attack a target in North Korea. We were armed with rockets. Targets tended to be small – perhaps a single building or a small bridge. No. 77 Squadron had a reputation for accuracy, and so we got the more difficult targets. I must say it took me a few operations before I reached the standard, but the Meteor was a very good ground attack aircraft. With its stubby wings it was not much affected by turbulence, and it was simply a matter of stabilising the sight on the target and waiting for the release height before pressing the button to send the rockets on their way. Ground fire was sometimes intense, and tracer ammunition is a bit off-putting at first—every bullet seems to be headed directly between the eyes before moving aside at the last moment. Add to that the fact that only one bullet in five had tracer, so you were more likely to be hit by one without tracer than one with. We soon learned to ignore it, because it never hit you. Well, almost never. I had a belly-tank holed on one occasion and had to jettison the tank. The aircraft felt much more lively without the belly-tank, but we needed the extra range so that was my only experience of flying without the belly-tank.

We slept in large tents, just like the ones you see in MASH. By the time I arrived, all the tents had floors and plywood walls and ceilings made from the boxes the US Sabre drop-tanks came in. Since the Sabres always jettisoned their drop-tanks over the Yalu River, these boxes were in plentiful supply. Each tent had a belly-stove fuelled by a drum of aviation turbine fuel (AVTUR), and outside was a fire bucket. Also outside was a slit trench, for protection in case of a raid. I had to make my own bed out of timbers from the ubiquitous drop-tank boxes and strips of rubber cut from old tubes.

Bob in Korea

The Squadron had more pilots than aeroplanes, and so we sometimes had a day off from operations. These days were filled by doing odd jobs around the place or simply reading a book. I discovered a book by Isaac Asimov in the US library, *Foundation* was the title, and I have been a keen science fiction reader ever since. I also decided to read the Bible, one chapter a day from beginning to end, so I could decide whether I believed in Christianity or not. This took almost four years altogether, and I was already married long before the end. I used the chaplains and others to discuss the many difficulties found, and gradually found myself a believer of sorts, although I still reject any suggestion that the Bible was dictated by God and therefore literally true. It is a collection of sacred writings by many authors, and often simply reflects the ideas of society 2,000 and more years ago. Still, it is important and contains much to inspire and guide our faith journey. But I digress.

One day, we noticed the refuelling tanker was filling the forty-four gallon drum beside our tent. It supplied the belly-stove through a small carburettor. We decided to test the stove in preparation for the coming winter. We turned on the tap and I took the lid off the burner, but noticed that the stove had quite a lot of water sitting in it—presumably from rain coming down the chimney.

"Don't worry," I said, "the heat will evaporate the water."

So we lit the stove by tossing in a match, only to discover that it was not water in the bottom but aviation fuel, which had leaked past the corroded tap and carburettor and pooled in the bottom of the heater. The fire became fierce. The chimney glowed red and then yellow. It was obvious that we had a big problem. I raced out and grabbed a bucket of sand. We managed to get the top off and throw the sand in and eventually put the fire out, but then we had the task of cleaning out the sand and repairing the carburettor before we could turn it back on. This took time, but after a week or so we finally had a working stove. Some others who tried out their stove were not so lucky. Three tents burned down in the US lines on the same day we nearly burned our tent down.

We did not have our own kitchens, so we were fed by the Americans. The sergeant pilots were made honorary members of the US Officers Mess, for rationing purposes, and we had to take off our sergeant's chevrons and simply wear our pilot wings. I even partnered our CO in the Officers Mess Bridge competition and we did very well, taking home prize money most weeks. We used the old-fashioned Culbertson bidding system, which we knew very well. The Americans all used the newly developed Goren system, which they did not understand very well—hence our success.

One of the things I remember about that time was the beer swilling and singing in the bar after a day of operations. A couple of verses will give the general impression:

> "It was midnight in Korea, all the pilots were in bed,
> When up spoke General Barkus and this is what he said,
> "Pilots, gentle pilots, how I love you one and all,
> Meteors, gentle Meteors" and the pilots shouted 'Balls!' "

… it goes downhill from there.

Or try this one:

> "Cruising down the Yalu at 490 per
> I called up my Flight Leader, 'O save me save me, sir.
> I've got two flak holes in my wing, my tanks are out of gas!
> Mayday, Mayday, Mayday, I've got six MIG's up my ass!' "

… it also goes downhill from there.

Back Home

Having survived the war, I was posted to Williamtown, on the staff of No. 2 Operational Training Unit—the unit that trained future fighter pilots. I took leave and Jenny and I were married in April 1954. We began our married life in a tiny two-bedroom flat at Nelson Bay, after a lovely honeymoon on Magnetic Island. We soon moved several times and ended up with a lovely roomy unit not far from our first one. Our first child, Mandi, was born in 1955.

CHAPTER 6
Married Life: Jenny

After we were married, our first posting was to RAAF Williamtown, in New South Wales. Bob was still too junior to qualify for a house on the base, so we ended up in Nelson Bay, which was just a little fishing village at that time.

For the first two weeks we stayed in an upstairs flat. One morning after Bob had left for work, I was headed for the outside toilet when a head appeared through the laundry window and looked me up and down.

"How old are you?" asked the owner of the head.

I lifted my left hand up to my chest in surprise, revealing my wedding ring, and replied, "I'm 19."

"Oh. You look about the same age as my daughter. I thought you'd be a good playmate for her," the woman said.

"How old is your daughter?" I asked.

"She's 14," came the response.

I was very short, after all.

The Dolls' House

After our stay in the upstairs flat we moved into what I called our dolls' house. It had four tiny rooms—a living room, two-bedrooms, and a kitchen, with an outside bathroom, toilet, and laundry, which housed a copper and hand wringer. The kitchen had a wood stove with two primus hobs. Fortunately, I knew how to do the Goldilocks test and tell the heat of the stove with my hand. There was no refrigerator when we first moved in.

Later, we had a kerosene refrigerator, which had to be turned upside down every three months. Doing the laundry in the copper and then putting everything through the hand wringer was always a chore, but the most memorable occasion was when I was heavily pregnant. I'd finished washing everything, including the sheets and towels, and hung it all out on the long line, which was held with a wooden prop. As I pushed the prop up it slipped off the line and hit me in the face. All the wet laundry ended up on the sandy black ground. I didn't have it in me to start over with the copper and the hand wringer, so I fetched buckets of water and washed the dirt off the clothes while they were still hung on the line.

Just before our first daughter, Amanda, arrived—15 months after our marriage—we moved into a bigger flat with an electric stove, an electric refrigerator, and an inside bathroom and laundry. We bought a Lightburn washing machine, which made my life far easier. However, not long after, the crankshaft of our Austin 7 car broke, and as we had spent our savings on the washing machine Bob had to spend several months getting lifts the twenty-one miles to work.

When Mandi was about six months old we moved into another upstairs flat, overlooking Port Stephen's Bay. It was a lovely flat with polished floorboards and resident Kookaburras, who came to the kitchen window to be fed at four o' clock each afternoon.

CHAPTER 7
Life in the RAAF: Bob

The RAAF was to be re-equipped with Avon Sabres, a variant of the North American F86, with an Avon engine—manufactured locally by the Government Aircraft Factory. In 1955 I was posted within No. 2OTU to the Sabre Trials Flight. Our task was to evaluate the Avon Sabre, test its top speed, highest altitude and so on, as well as to write the pilot's manual. It was the glamour unit of the RAAF. As a flight sergeant I was the most junior member, and, as such, my photo (such as the one below) appeared in the papers from time to time.

Sabre Pilot

In 1956, I was posted to the Central Flying School at East Sale to do the Instructor's Course. From there to Point Cook, Melbourne, to be an instructor on Wirraways. What a let down after Sabres!

Then we were moved to Pearce, in Western Australia, and began the first jet courses flying Vampire Mk 33, a dual-control version of the Vampire. I was nearly posted to No. 24 Squadron at Malalla, South Australia, but was sent instead to the Department of Air in Melbourne. It was my first desk job. I wanted to return to flying, so when I was offered a chance to go to America to learn to fly helicopters I jumped at it. Unfortunately it was an unaccompanied posting, so I was apart from my wife and children for the six months of the course.

I was then posted to the newly formed No. 9 Squadron, based at Fairbairn, which shared an aerodrome with the civilian Canberra Airport. We received the new UH-1 Iroquois helicopters. At first, our task was to supply search and rescue helicopters to bases with single-seat aircraft, but soon found ourselves doing mainly Army support. I was sent for three months to Darwin, to set up the search and rescue unit. The others in the squadron went one month at a time

During the time at Fairbairn I wrote the Flying Instructors Course for the helicopters.

But I also recall a funny incident at Laverton, Victoria. We were to participate in a race against other RAAF aircraft. Being in helicopters, we were allowed to take off first. As a laugh, my superior officer instructed me to hide behind the tallest building and reappear to win the race, which I did. But as I was shutting down the engine, a little boy came up to me in tears, saying, "You cheated! My daddy was winning!" I told him it was okay, that they would declare me as cheating.

Unfotunately, they failed to do so and I was declared the winner.

CHAPTER 8

RAAF Family Life: Jenny

After more than two years there, during which time Bob had been flying Vampires before moving on to the Sabre trails flight, he was posted to Sale for the instructor's course. By this time I was pregnant with our second child, who was due on the 15th of December, 1956. Bob's course finished on the 14th of December, so I stayed with my family in Melbourne, with Bob coming up for weekends. After Ian arrived on the 15th, we spent Christmas with the family. Bob was then posted to Point Cook in Melbourne, although we ended up renting a house miles away, in Canterbury. However, by this time we had bought a small, and very old, Morris 840, and not long after the move I got my licence, which was just as well, as after a short time as Bob was sent to RAAF Rathmines at Lake Macquarie for three months, on another course.

Ten months after moving to Canterbury Bob was posted to Pearce, in Western Australia, as a flying instructor on Vampires. The Morris would not have made it all the way to Perth, so it was sold. For the first three months that we were in Western Australia we rented a house at Greenmount, about twenty-one miles from Pearce RAAF base, after which time we moved onto the base. It rained very often during the time we were living in Greenmount, and there was plenty of red dirt in the back garden, so I had some interesting red nappies to wash from a very active little boy. Once we had moved onto the base at Pearce Ian was confidently toddling, and became a master of escaping the yard. As we had the Main Northern Highway to our east, and bush with a dam to the west, it was a job to keep track of him. Every time I thought I'd blocked him from getting out, he found another way. His best effort at escapology was attempting to climb a tennis court fence while we were having lunch at a cricket match. All the children had been shut into the tennis court, with the older children watching the younger ones. I had to talk him down, as the adults were too heavy to climb up after him without shaking him off the fence.

There was also an air show there one day. I was very pregnant with number three and had taken the other two small children over to watch the air show. It was windy, so I moved in front of the nearby building to shelter. I heard an RAAF officer say that one more knot of wind and we would have to cancel the aerobatic display. Then he added, "Do you think we should cancel?" Bob was in the Number 4 position of the 4 Aces Aerobatic Team, one of the hardest and most dangerous positions of the formation, so my feeling was to poke my head into the officer's cubicle and tell him "Yes!" but I refrained. Thankfully, the whole display went very well, including the 4 Aces.

The 4 Aces Aerobatic Flying Team

Our third child arrived in April 1959, two weeks before we were due to arrive in Melbourne for ten months before going on to Canberra. Bob had come back to help me move, as it was too much for me to manage on my own with three children under four years old, and the baby being only two weeks. She had been due the day we were to move, but had decided to arrive a bit early.

After our ten months in Melbourne, and now owning a Hillman Husky station sedan we arrived in Canberra, to a brand-new house without a garden. Bob went back to Melbourne, leaving me with an asthmatic child, no telephone, a boggy drive and no idea where to find a doctor. Luck was with us, as she didn't have a bad attack of asthma while he was away.

Four years later, in 1962, after Bob had gone to USA for six months to learn to fly helicopters, we used two very small reel-to-reel tape recorders to communicate. During the six months that Bob was away, the RAAF did not get in touch with me to see how I was managing on my own with three small children.

Not long after he returned to Australia, he was sent on another officer's training course, this time at Rathmines in New South Wales. As the course was set to run for four months, we decided that the children and I would spend the first week staying in Sydney with Bob's mother, Mavis, while Bob found a place for us to stay at Lake Macquarie for the rest of the course. After six weeks with no success, and Bob making the journey back to Sydney each weekend, we decided to drive up with the children, so that I could look for somewhere for us to stay while Bob was working. We drove up on the Sunday, and the hotel was booked until the Wednesday, which was all we could afford. One child became sick in the middle of Sunday night, and so Monday morning was taken up with a visit to the doctor. After that, I went to see the real estate agent, who laughed at me, saying nothing was available. In desperation, I put an ad in the local paper, and the following morning two offers came in—a share house for five pounds a week, and a boatshed for four pounds a week. I saw the share house first. The accommodation was a living room, with sofa bed which Bob and I would share, plus two small rubber seats on a window seat for the older children to sleep on, and the baby would have to make do with her pram. The rules were that we had to vacate the room on Sundays, as that was their family time in the living room. There was nowhere for us to put our clothes, and I had to provide my assurance that the children wouldn't wake my husband before six o' clock in the morning.

After that, I went to see the boatshed near the end of the lake. It had been divided into three, with two single beds and a cot for the baby and a double bed with a small hanging place for clothes for Bob and me. There was a Primus burner and a small stove, a sink, and a table and chairs. They explained that the bathroom wasn't finished and we would have to use their bathroom, which was on the outside of their house near the boatshed. All this for four pounds a week!

We had a great time in the boatshed. Bob was only home for Wednesday and Friday nights, and from Saturday morning until late Sunday afternoon. While we were at the boatshed, two violent prisoners, Dugan and Mears, escaped from prison and were thought to be hiding in the bush nearby. Fortunately, they were quickly captured and we were able to sleep easier.

Whilst in the helicopter squadron, Bob wrote the instructor's course papers, for which he was awarded the Air Force Cross.

He was also the first to fly a helicopter for flood rescue in Queensland, where he had some interesting adventures. In the three years he was with the helicopter squadron, he was away more than any other pilot—a total of two out of the three years.

Flood Work

In the early 1960's, Bob took part in helicopter training exercises in New Guinea for a couple of weeks. When the crew returned, they dropped Bob off in Townsville so that he could fly a spare chopper back to Canberra the following morning.

At 2 am, when Bob was fast asleep, an orderly officer woke him to ask how long would it take for Bob to fly to Adavale, in Queensland, and pick up 11 men who were stranded on the roof of the hotel, after a flash flood.

Bob's first question was, 'Where is Adavale?'

'I don't know, sir,' came the reply.

After hunting in the map room, an old German pre-World War Two map of the world was found, which showed where in Queensland Adavale was situated. Bob worked out that if they took off at first light they should reach Adavale by about 5 pm, although it was going to be tight as far as distance went when it came to refuelling.

The map showed only one distinctive landmark en route, about halfway between Maryborough and Roma. This landmark comprised a river with a billabong and a road going north south. After refuelling at Maryborough, Bob set off towards Roma, but the landmark appeared 3 times instead of once, the 3rd time would mean not enough fuel to reach Roma. Bob decided that he would keep flying until the 20-minute warning light came on, and then stop at the next station they flew over to buy fuel. The warning light came on, and the crew began scanning the countryside for a station, but there was nothing but bush as far as the eye could see. When Roma finally came in sight, Bob managed into the airport literally on a wing and a prayer.

They continued on to Adavale, making it before sunset, and discovered that the men had spent two days on the roof with little more than the top shelf spirits from the pub to sustain them. The men were taken to the police station, and Bob flew on to Quilpie to rest for the night, with more rescues planned for the following day.

Rigby and a QLD Rescue

On the way to Quilpie the crew spotted two men perched on top of an old shed, with water swirling round the building almost up to the roof. The engineer was lowered down in order to winch the men up and take them to safety, but the men refused to leave without their dogs, and as dogs and choppers are not a good mix Bob was not able to take them. Instead, Bob flew as low as he could, and they lowered a self-inflating life raft for the men and the dogs to use.

On arriving at Quilpie, Bob and the crew were greeted by a large number of newspaper, radio and television reporters and film crews. Bob agreed to speak to one reporter, on condition that they shared the story with all the other news crews.

After that, they went to the Imperial Hotel for a beer, a meal, and a bed for the night. In the bar, there was a dogfight in progress with bets being taken. The next morning they set off for a homestead where a mother was stranded with her two children, a cat, a budgerigar and a pet galah. The engineer was winched down to find out if they would like to be helicoptered out, but the woman wouldn't leave, as she was worried the cat would eat the birds. It was finally agreed that the cat could come as the birds had food there. The engineer picked the cat up by the scruff of the neck. The cat was thoroughly unimpressed by this indignity, and clawed through the engineer's flying suit, and his arm, before taking off.

After this, the woman decided that she would handle the galah herself, so she put the budgie in its cage and the galah up her jumper. The children were winched up first, followed by their mother. The crewman on the winch was feeling quite pleased with himself as he reached his hands around the woman's body to pull her into the chopper—until the galah poked it's head out of her jumper and gave him a vicious bite! He was feeling quite sorry for himself, until the engineer was winched up with his arm still bleeding.

The next job was to check on the men and their dogs, to see if they'd made it off the roof of the tin shed. On arriving, they discovered the raft had been very neatly tied to the shed, and as it contained emergency supplies Bob was satisfied they were going to be fine.

On they went, this time to two men stranded in a big truck on a small sand island in the middle of a river. Bob landed on another small island nearby and was about to shout over to the men to ask if they wanted to be rescued, but he was beaten to it, when one of the men shouted over, asking Bob if he needed help. Although the water was lapping at the truck tyres, once it had been established that in Bob's view it was the two men who were in need of assistance, rather than the RAAF helicopter crew, the men reassured Bob that they were fine, and that the water was slowly subsiding. Bob then shouted over, 'What about food?'

'Do you want some, mate?' came the reply.

The rest of the rescues went without a hitch, and they managed to help a number of people over the next few days.

Family Time

Shortly after moving to Lyons in the Woden Valley, we attended a very large fete in the grounds of the Governor General's home. As the fete was finishing and we had time to look around, we saw a very large marquee with a label saying, 'For Sale'.

It was a two-pole marquee, and we decided then and there that it would be perfect for camping holidays, so we bought it. We divided one-third of the marquee off into bedrooms for the children. The rest of the tent was living quarters, which doubled as our bedroom at night. It proved to be a very comfortable and happy arrangement.

One of our earliest camps in it was at Narooma. However, we arrived a little late in the Christmas holidays, after having had Christmas at home. There were very few spots left to fit our big tent, but we found a nice green spot backing onto the golf course.

In the middle of the night it rained. Not long after this, a voice called out, "Mum, I've got something in my eye."

"I'll look at it in the morning," I muttered sleepily.

"It needs looking at now," came Ian's insistent reply, so I stepped off the air bed into several inches water.

On investigation, I found that Ian had a tick lodged right next to his eye. I felt panicky, but Bob was calm.

"We can't use a match to burn it out," he pointed out, "so let's try dipping tweezers in Solyptol and see if that works."

Thankfully, it did. We are all standing in several inches of water throughout the impromptu medical procedure. The next morning, some kind campers helped to move our tent to a dry spot. We should have known better than to camp on such low-lying ground, with our background in Scouting and Guiding!

On another camping trip to the coast I was taking rubbish out to the bin when I slipped down a very small slope in the darkness and landed on my backside. It was extremely painful, and I had to rest for a few days before I could face the drive home.

Once home I visited the doctor, who said my coccyx was either badly bruised or broken. An X-ray would be needed to confirm which it was. I asked what would happen if the X-ray showed it was broken. He replied that nothing would happen, other than I would know how long the pain would last.

"How long will the pain last?" I enquired.

"About six months for the bruising to subside, and up to two years if it is broken," he replied.

I declined the X-ray. The pain lasted for around eighteen months, lessening over time, and has not given me any trouble since.

Shortly after arriving home from a camping trip, I was cross with our youngest, who was then just three years old. She stamped her foot and asked, "Why can't we go back and live properly in the tent, instead of this brick house?"

I guess I was more relaxed on holiday.

We had many enjoyable camping trips in that tent, and only sold it when we were moving to Edinburgh in 1974, by which time it was definitely showing its age.

A Birthday To Remember
On our eldest daughter's ninth birthday, I baked the cake and Bob iced and decorated it, as had been the tradition in our household since we were first married, when I gladly handed over the responsibility to him after struggling to ice our first Christmas cake. From then on, he decorated all the family birthday, Christmas and wedding cakes.

On this particular birthday, we had given three children the day off school so that we could go up to the snow. They still talk about that day as being only one of two days they were ever given off school—the other being for the moon landing.

I was heavily pregnant with our fourth child when we went to the snow, but we had a great time sledding on a small hill. Then it came time for the cake! We got it out of the car and Bob placed eight candles on the cake. As he was lighting them a little voice piped up, "Daddy I am nine, not eight."

Quick as a flash Bob lit a match to make up the number, holding it until it was nearly burning his fingers.

CHAPTER 9

Malaysia & Vietnam: Bob

In March 1965, I was posted to No. 5 Squadron at Butterworth RAAF Base, Malaysia, to be the Squadron Flying Instructor. After a year of very interesting flying, the Squadron was moved to Canberra, but the pilots and almost all the ground crew were posted to No. 9 Squadron in Vietnam. Thus began what came to be known as the '9 to 5 job', as pilots were shuttled between the two squadrons.

No. 9 Squadron was based in Vung Tau, and was tasked with the support of the Australian Task force based in Nui Dat, about twenty minutes flying away. We carried troops into battle and removed them from battles, too. We were often fired at, but very seldom suffered any hits. The Viet Cong were trained to fire one helicopter length ahead of a chopper, which would result in a hit if the aircraft were flying at certain height/speed combinations—which we studiously avoided. I even saw one Viet Cong soldier aim ahead of my helicopter when it was sitting on the ground! My gunner shot him before he learned the error of his ways.

I was in Bribie Battle, which had a consequence later, as well as taking the wounded out of Long Tan Battle the night of that battle.

After nine months in Vietnam, I was posted, along with Max Hayes, another flight lieutenant and flying instructor, back to 5 Squadron, based in Canberra, to train the next generation of helicopter pilots for the war. I was senior, so was Temporary

CO and had four students, while Max was Training Flight Commander, and had five students. I am not sure how we did it, but at the end of nine months when help arrived we were both physically and mentally exhausted. We were given leave, and I found out later our papers were marked 'not to be recalled even in a national emergency'. As it happened, Harold Holt went missing at sea during our leave, but neither of us was recalled for the search. Sadly, Max succumbed to the strain and committed suicide.

During my time as 5 Squadron Commander, an airman came to see me and informed me that his Father had died, and there was no way he could reach East Gippsland by public transport in time for the funeral. I told him I would look into it for him. As a result, I rang one of the two senior officers who could give me permission to take him by helicopter to Gippsland, and class it as a training exercise. As it was a Wednesday afternoon, the officer in Canberra was out playing golf, so I tried the other officer at Penrith. Unfortunately, it was the same story. In spite of my inability to get the required permission, I made the decision to take the airman down to East Gippsland. Several weeks later I received a request asking me to explain the incident. On explanation, I was told in no uncertain terms that I should not have taken the airman, but as the officer was about to ring off he said he would have done the same thing.

As a family, we were fortunate enough to be based in Canberra, either at No. 5 Squadron for at the Department of Air or at Edinburgh. In July 1974 I was posted to Edinburgh Base Squadron for the remainder of my RAAF career. I retired in 1978 with the rank of Wing Commander.

CHAPTER 10

Malaysia, Vietnam & Australia: Jenny

In March 1965, Bob became involved in the Malaysian confrontation. It was soon after we arrived that I found myself being trained as a Brownie Leader, as my eldest daughter was disgusted to find that there was a Cub Scout group for her brother, but no Brownies for her.

We lived in Butteworth whilst Bob was in Vietnam. One day he came home on a three-day visit sporting a very healthy moustache. Our daughter, who was 5 or 6 at the time, told him that if he ever came home with that moustache he would not be allowed in the door.

For anyone who has not been in Malaya you may not know about the shrews there. About 4 inches long, or 10 centimetres, they are very vicious capable of biting a finger off. Bob had been given a beautiful 5ft blowpipe and darts by the aborigines in the North Central part of Malaysia. One night a shrew had a housecat bailed up. The shrew was caught under the fence and the cat was too terrified to move. Both were making a loud racket, so Bob took the blowpipe and inserted an un-poisoned dart. He hit the back of the cat who took off while the shrew finally struggled under the fence and took off after the cat, who had by now disappeared and hopefully escaped.

Later, when we returned to Australia by ship, Bob went to customs with our cane cases and his 5ft blowpipe. Gone much longer than expected, he explained that the customs had refused to let him enter with the blowpipe as it was 'a dangerous weapon', but he thought the darts had all been lost. As he had come straight from Vietnam, I had arranged the move, and and the darts were actually in the cane case at his feet!

When the Squadron was sent to Vietnam, Bob and a sergeant were left to pack everything destined to go back to Australia. Bob announced that they were not going to report anything missing. This meant that if they found only one pair of pliers instead of two, there would suddenly be two broken half pairs of pliers. Once they had finished packing everything, the only thing missing was a tab bender—a tool made to adjust the ends of the rotor on the helicopter. So off Bob went to a section who could make such things, and duly put in the box and ticked off. Sometime later in Vietnam Bob received a letter asking why there were two tab benders in the box. The 'missing' tab bender had been put in the box but not ticked off.

In 1966, Bob was posted to fly helicopters in the Vietnam War. They lived in an old French villa at Vung Tau. Every night bats flew right out an open window, coming back early in the morning. As they made such a noise and a mess, the window was duly shut. The next morning, dead bats started falling as they hit the window. The problem, however, was not solved. Bats were still in the ceiling. So after another night of bats hitting the window trying to get out, the window remained open for the remainder of our stay.

This was originally scheduled to be for twelve months from June to June, but as Bob was needed back in Canberra in March 1967 he finished early. We sailed from Malaysia to Australia, which was lucky, as Bob was very tired after his time in Vietnam, and it gave him a short break before arriving back to a big job as Acting Commanding Officer and Chief Flying Instructor in Canberra.

We had purchased a house in Canberra before we went overseas, but when we returned we quickly realised it was too small for our family, even though we had added a large family room before we went away. We were lucky to find a split-level house that we could afford, as prices were suddenly going up.

During our time in Canberra, we had all three children at a private schools, so I took various part-time jobs to help cover the fees. We stayed in Canberra until 1974, with Bob ending up as Commanding Officer back at the Helicopter Squadron.

It was during this time that our 12-year-old daughter, Fiona, arrived home late from school one day. She was due for her piano lesson and I was cross with her for being late. On the way home from the lesson she explained that she was late after school because she had been accosted by a man on her way to the bus stop. She said, 'I got away and ran to the end of the street to see him getting in his car, so I wrote his car number on my hand.' We went straight to the police and he was caught.

After Canberra, we were posted to Edinburgh RAAF Base in South Australia, in July 1974. This meant leaving Ian and Fiona at boarding school in Canberra and taking Ailsa with us to. Our eldest daughter, Mandi, had already married.

The Edinburgh posting was intended to be for only eighteen months, but we ended up staying until December 1978, as Bob was asked each year if he would he stay on for another year. I had never known that to happen. The squadron grew each year, and by the time we left there were about 400 personnel.

One of my favourite sections to visit was the guard dogs. We had the best guard dog in the RAAF at this time. He lost a canine tooth in practice one day, and the men thought he would have to be put down as he was getting old. The dentist offered to replace it with a gold tooth, though he wasn't sure if the old dog would survive the operation. Thankfully, he did, and he became very proud of his new gleaming tooth, showing it off at any opportunity. But he was not so successful the following year after losing a second canine tooth.

Court Marshall

Bob told me that whilst at Edinburgh a very good corporal had hit a lazy airman on the nose. This was a Court Marshall offence—something Bob could not deal with himself. However, he knew from a training story that he might be able to give him a Plea in Bar of a trial.

The training story was of a lieutenant who went to receive a DSO from the king, during the Second World War. When he went to receive his DSO, the lieutenant was accompanied by an escort. The king asked why the lieutenant had an escort, and was told he was on a Court Marshall. The king asked what he had done. On being told, he said, 'That was very naughty. Don't do it again,' while wagging a finger at the lieutenant. At his Court Marshall his defence claimed that the king had punished him, so he was pardoned with a Plea in Bar of trial

Bob hoped he could do the same for this good corporal, so called him into his office and gave him a very severe dressing down. As the corporal left, Bob saw the airman smirking and so called him in, and gave him an equally severe dressing down. The result was that the corporal got off his Court Marshall, and the lazy airman pulled his socks up, with each man reaching the highest rank attainable for them.

In December 1978 Bob retired from the RAAF, and we bought a lovely old bluestone house at 192 King William Rd,

Hyde Park. After leaving the Airforce, Bob entered Parkin Wesley College to study to become a Uniting Church Minister. At that time, the College was on King William Rd. I typed his theological essays for him on an old typewriter.

While Bob was studying, I continued to be involved with the Girl Guides, and was given an additional job, as the Disaster Coordinator for South Australian Girl Guides. In 1981, when we had the first Ash Wednesday bushfire, I oversaw the food preparation and delivery to the disaster-relief workers.

Commanding Officer, Base Squadron, Edinburgh SA

Ordination, 1981

Bob was ordained as a Uniting Church Minister in December 1981, and in January 1982 we moved to Bordertown, where he was the UCA minister for Bordertown, Padthaway, Mundulla, Buckingham and Wolsely. We stayed in Bordertown until January 1985, when Bob became the Frontier Service Patrol Padre for the Murchison Patrol, in Western Australia.

So Long

Our Bob and our Jenny are going out West,
And we say, "Fare thee well!" as we wish them the best,
They've found a place of love right in our hearts,
And we're sad as they leave us to go to far away parts.

So Long, It's Been Good To Know You,
So Long, It's Been Good To Know You,
So Long, It's Been Good To Know You,
We'll Follow You With Interest And Love In Our Hearts,
As You Serve Him In Far Away Parts.

The Guides and the Brownies are close to her heart,
And Jenny has led them by doing her part,
Embroiderers will miss her, her needle and thread,
As she sewed and embroidered a quilt for the bed.

So Long, It's Been Good To Know You,
So Long, It's Been Good To Know You,
So Long, It's Been Good To Know You,
We'll Follow You With Interest And Love In Our Hearts,
As You Serve Him In Far Away Parts.

The oldies at Charla have loved Bob dearly,
As he called to give them a message clearly,
He had time to talk to them, frail as they be,
And they all felt blessed as he shared faithfully.

So Long, It's Been Good To Know You,
So Long, It's Been Good To Know You,
So Long, It's Been Good To Know You,
We'll Follow You With Interest And Love In Our Hearts,
As You Serve Him In Far Away Parts.

LIVING ON A WING AND A PRAYER

The F.M. Radio will not be the same,
When they leave us, our Bob and our Jenny by name,
The Fraternal and Rotary have been a part,
Of the interests of Bob that he's taken to heart.

So Long, It's Been Good To Know You,
So Long, It's Been Good To Know You,
So Long, It's Been Good To Know You,
We'll Follow You With Interest And Love In Our Hearts,
As You Serve Him In Far Away Parts.

The meetings and meetings and meetings galore,
Have taken their time – then taken some more,
But neither a growl nor a grump nor a sigh
Was heard from them ever by you or I.

So Long, It's Been Good To Know You,
So Long, It's Been Good To Know You,
So Long, It's Been Good To Know You,
We'll Follow You With Interest And Love In Our Hearts,
As You Serve Him In Far Away Parts.

Our Bob and our Jenny are going out west ,
We say "Fare thee well' as we wish them the best,
They've found a place of love right in our hearts.
And we're sad as they leave us to go to far away parts.

So Long, It's Been Good To Know You,
So Long, It's Been Good To Know You,
So Long, It's Been Good To Know You,
We'll Follow You With Interest And Love In Our Hearts,
As You Serve Him In Far Away Parts.

CHAPTER 11

Becoming A Patrol Minister: Bob

Sometime in the middle of 1983, Frontier Services sent out a circular letter to every Uniting Church Minister, asking us to consider patrol ministry.

There were a lot of vacancies coming up for January 1984, but I had only been at Bordertown for eighteen months and felt that it would not be fair to leave so soon. There was only one job that really interested me: the Tennant Barkly Patrol, which would be vacant from January 1985. It was based in a truck-mounted mobile home called the Padre's Palace. I talked to Jenny about it and she was interested. We both love camping and we both love the outback.

However, Bordertown was a very busy Parish and we more or less forgot about it until about a month later when we were in Perth on holidays. We were visiting some old friends, Rev. Ian MacPherson and his wife Judi. During our conversation, Ian asked me what I would do when my three years were up at Bordertown. I mentioned to him that the circular letter had interested us, and especially the Tennant Barkly Patrol.

Ian is not a man to let grass grow under his feet. He wrote to Rev. Gray Birch, then General Secretary of Frontier Services, and said we were interested in patrol ministry. He mentioned that I had been an RAAF pilot and strongly recommended us. Two weeks later, when we got home to Bordertown, there was a letter from Gray waiting for us. In it, he asked us to meet him to discuss patrol ministry. I rang and arranged to meet him at the coming Synod meeting in Adelaide.

As it happened, Jenny was in Darwin when the meeting took place, but I did not think there was much urgency about making a decision, and approached the meeting as very much a preliminary exploration. We talked for a few minutes and got on very well. Imagine my surprise when Gray took the ball and opened with a bouncer.

"How would you like to go to Meekatharra?" said he.

"Where's that?" says I.

"In the middle of Western Australia," Gray explains, before throwing another bouncer, "It's a flying patrol and I hear you're a pilot."

I had to admit that I was, but said it had been a while since I'd flown and that I was fifty-five, which was getting on for a pilot. Not only that, but I didn't have a civil licence. They were good excuses, but then I made a small mistake.

"I don't suppose I would have a lot of trouble getting a civilian licence, but I don't know how long I could keep up to the aircrew medical standard."

In no time, Gray suggested a series of steps to test whether this was what God wanted us to do. First, to see what Jenny felt. Second, to have a medical examination. If all went well, then Jenny and I could fly to Meekatharra and have a look at the place, all expenses paid and no strings attached. Then, if everything was to our satisfaction, I could just get my licence and go. Gray thought it could all be done in a few weeks, and he wanted us to start at Meekatharra in January 1984. I told him that I would not be available until January 1985, as I wanted to finish my three-year appointment at Bordertown. Gray reluctantly agreed. I must say that by the time he had finished, I was quite enthusiastic.

The first hurdle was telling Jenny. I rang her and asked, "How would you like to learn to fly?" I knew she had always wanted to learn to fly, so I thought this was a clever ploy.

"What's the catch?" she said. So much for my clever ploy! I explained all about it and she was keen to find out more. I had the medical and everything was fine. The doctor said I passed with flying colours. I am unsure whether the pun was intended or not.

Then we had to find a time when we could go to Meekatharra. We decided it would have to be in January, after our youngest daughter's wedding. We have heard since that Gray was sure we would not like Meekatharra in January and expected us to decline the appointment. However, despite the extreme heat (it reached forty-three degrees on both the days we were there), we loved what we saw. The only problem was that the aeroplane was not there, and nobody seemed to know where it was. I rang the synod secretary, and he said he would find out where it was and make sure we were able to look at it. He was as good as his word. He found out that it had had a fairly serious accident and was being repaired in Northam, about eighty kilometres out of Perth. We were taken there on the last day of our trip, and I was able to see what a good aeroplane it was: a Cessna 182 with only about 1,500 hours on the clock and a comprehensive radio fit. It even had a simple autopilot, although we later found out it was quite hopeless—as I had never used an autopilot we never missed it. When we got home we rang Gray and said we would like to accept the appointment, but not until January 1985. He confirmed the appointment by return mail.

Meekatharra

Next, we had to decide how to tell the Parish at Bordertown. We decided to do it straight away so that they would have ten months to find a successor. Somebody asked me afterwards what we would have done if I had failed to get a civilian licence. It had never occurred to me!

So, off I went to the nearest aero club, at Nhill Victoria, to get my unrestricted private pilot's licence. I took all my logbooks with me and the young instructor was most impressed.

"I don't know who will be teaching who how to fly," he said.

I assured him that he would be the teacher. "I haven't flown a fixed wing aeroplane for twenty-five years!" His jaw dropped.

"That was before I was born!" he said.

Really, the only trouble I had was relearning how to land. The last 16 years of my RAAF career had been flying either helicopters or the 'mahogany bomber'—RAAF slang for a desk in an office. The technique for landing a helicopter is totally different from landing an ordinary plane like a Cessna 152.

It took about twelve hours to get my flying completely up to scratch, including two flight tests. In the meantime, I had to pass eight exams, which I did at the rate of one every week, except for the last one which took two goes. What with one thing and another, it took eight months to squeeze all of this into my parish commitments, but I really enjoyed it. It was a great feeling to be back in the air. By the end of September we could hardly wait to get to the west.

It only remained to decide what to take, what to put into storage, and what to sell, give away or throw away. The experience we'd had with moving during my time in the Air Force, with a total of nineteen moves in twenty-seven years, was very useful. We had become very good at moving, although we never actually got to the stage of liking it.

Soon, the manse became infected with the cardboard box disease. This is a very insidious condition. It begins with a few boxes hidden here and there. Then the boxes begin to multiply. When there is nowhere left to hide them, they begin to line the corridors and obstruct movement. Finally, they fill every available space from floor-to-head height. And then the removals truck arrives to take them to the destinations carefully shown on each box.

The move was complicated by the fact that the truck which was to take our stuff out had the furniture and boxes of our successors on board. Fortunately, it was a dry day and, for the first time in our removals history, the truck turned up on time. All went smoothly and we were able to leave for the west the next day in our near-new Nissan Urvan, towing our old faithful box trailer. We had packed a selection of things in the vehicle and trailer so that, if our furniture was late getting to Meekatharra, we could camp in the house until it arrived. This turned out to be a wise precaution as our furniture arrived in Meekatharra two weeks after we did!

We spent six days on the road, including a stopover for three nights in Perth. There, we were put up by Rev. Ron Smith. Ron was the WA synod secretary at the time, and he wanted to give us an orientation into the synod and the patrol. He introduced us to lots of people and we were made to feel very welcome. One of the people Ron introduced us to was Rev. Don McKaskill, who had been the patrol padre for the Murchison patrol in the 1950's. His exploits in the Tiger Moth were legendary, and were still spoken of by the old timers who had known and loved him when we moved up to Meekatharra. He and his wife Jean became very dear friends.

Perth, Headed For Meekatharra

We arrived in Meekatharra in the middle of January. It was hot. The house had been without tenants for a whole year, and when we moved in it had become the home of mice, spiders, ants and enormous cockroaches. The locals had been given a few days notice of our coming, and had vacuumed and dusted, put milk and bread and a few biscuits in the fridge, and generally tidied up around the place. We were extremely grateful for this, but we still had plenty to do.

The house was sparsely furnished, but it had air conditioners in all three bedrooms as well as in the lounge and kitchen. We went down to the shops and bought the pest control stuff we needed, and battle commenced. It was not long before we had most of the unwanted guests evicted, but the battle with the Singapore ants took almost a year before we got rid of the last of them.

A member of the church handed over a mountain of mail and the key to PO Box 14, which had a few more letters in it. Most of the mountain was ecclesiastical or other junk mail, and/or out of date. All of these were consigned to the round filing system—also know as the bin. Only two were of any lasting importance: a letter from Gray Birch welcoming us to the Frontier Services team, and a letter from Paroo Station inviting us to the annual cricket match on Australia Day.

We accepted the invitation, and I set about the task of collecting the aeroplane from Perth. I flew down to Perth on the local air service and spent a couple of days buying the necessary maps and charts, having my licence endorsed for the Cessna 182, and arranging the ongoing maintenance of the aeroplane. Then I flew the Cessna back to Meekatharra.

Every month, I had to send a report of my activities to the Sydney office. The first of my monthly reports to Rev. Gray Birch, Secretary of Frontier Services, was written on the 1st of February 1985, and included the following:

Dear Gray,

Removal

The removal was arranged through SA Synod and went according to plan. It might have been possible to get an earlier uplift if we had hooked into their system from the start, but Kyle was most cooperative. In retrospect I'm glad we had 10 days clear to pack. The farewells at Bordertown prevented any meaningful attempt to pack until 31 Dec 84. Unfortunately the furniture has still not arrived. It is promised for 5th February. This means that we can't hope to make much progress on our programmes of ministry until about 12th. (In this heat it will take at least a week to unpack).

The Manse

The local people had made some attempt to make the place habitable and it is to their credit that only 3 shrubs died and the place was secure and tidy. They had put milk and margarine in the fridge and tea and biscuits in the cupboards. However, the 12 months without tenants left a legacy of minor problems. The lawn was dead.

The trickle watering system had developed a number of leaks and is still not fully repaired. Every tap in the house leaked and this had caused a lot of white deposits mixed with red dust to encrust sink, shower recess, hand basin, bath etc. The cistern dripped water continuously into the toilet bowl. I have replaced washers and repaired the cistern. Jenny has just about finished removing the encrustations. There was red dust in the carpets and on the tiles and linoleum. The vacuum cleaner has worked overtime. The biggest task is trying to regain control of the garden. This will take a while but we have made a good start. The only other problem was blocked gutters which I have cleared out this day in driving rain so we could fill the rain water tanks. We have taken four trailer loads of junk and weeds to the tip. About two more should finish it. The general condition of the building, carpets, appliances etc is good.

Initial ideas on ministry to congregations

I conducted worship at Meekatharra on 27 Jan. 19 people were in attendance and I was told many were still on holidays. I hear that 3 young men have been running services and their efforts were appreciated. At least 2 are willing to continue to run services when needed. Next Sunday I intend to be at Wiluna (provided that the road or strip is open by then) and the last Sunday of February I will try to do Meekatharra, Cue and Mount Magnet. These days selected themselves and I will try to get a more rational programme organised from the beginning of March. My aim will be to preach twice a month at Meekatharra and once a month at the other centres. The fifth Sundays will be negotiable. This will mean only two sermons to write every month which should release me to do more visiting than I otherwise could. Please note that these ideas are only preliminary.

Aircraft Matters

The main considerations are covered in my letter of last week. However, I have been working out more secure ways to tether the aircraft to cope with the very strong winds we seem to get here. At present I am using improvised nose wheel chocks, but I feel that it would be wise to have proper chocks made up for all 3 wheels. These would consist of 3 pieces of 11/2" angle iron welded together to make a U shape. I will get a quote before I go ahead.

Ministry to Stations

Last Monday (28th January) Jenny and I were invited to go to the annual cricket match between East Gascoyne Pastoralists and Graziers Association and the towns people of Leinster, Wiluna and Meekatharra. It was a 19-a-side match played in 40-degree heat but was a serious sporting event with medals and trophies etc. Much to my surprise, I found myself playing (I made

2 runs and took one wicket). It was a great day held at Paroo Station – about 40 miles from Wiluna. Jenny and I discovered how much people appreciated the chance to talk about basic beliefs and philosophies. Not all were Christian but the Church commands great respect. We flew in, stayed the night and flew out the next day. A feature of the two days was that our hosts gathered everyone for worship after dinner AND before breakfast. The Anglican bloke from Leinster (Rev Don Miller) and I shared the services. He runs a service in Wiluna every month and we agreed to coordinate our services so that Wiluna would have 2 services a month. On Tuesday afternoon Graham and Di Forsythe of 'Three Rivers' Station called to see us and invited us to visit them. This was to have taken place yesterday and I had arranged through RFDS to let other stations up that way know we would visit them. However, Cyclone Gertie intervened and all roads and strips in the area are closed. We look forward to getting down to it properly when our furniture is unpacked.

CHAPTER 12
Outback Ministry: Jenny

Although the name has changed over time, from patrol padre to patrol minister to bush chaplain, the role has remained the same, and is founded on a long history of outback ministry. The Reverend John Flynn, founder of the Australian Inland Mission, sent his first minister out on patrol in 1912. This first patrol padre was the Rev. Bruce Ploughman, and he set off from Oodnadatta in December 1912 mounted on a camel. Over time, the number of patrols increased and the means of transport improved.

In 1977, after the Uniting Church of Australia was formed from the union of the Presbyterian, Methodist and Congregational Churches, the name of the organisation was changed from the Australian Inland Mission to Frontier Services.

At the time we were in the Murchison patrol, there were a total of twenty-five patrols, covering eighty percent of Australia. In the nine years that we were with the Murchison patrol, we were always made welcome wherever we went, on the stations, in the mines, in the Indigenous communities and the small towns within our boundaries. The long history of outback ministry meant that people understood our purpose, and accepted us.

The bush chaplain's role is not only to tend to the day-to-day pastoral needs of the people living within their boundaries, but to represent these people's needs to the decision-makers. Every month, the bush chaplain sends a full report to Frontier

Services in Sydney, detailing the services they have conducted, along with how many kilometres they have covered, by land and air. As a result, the Sydney office has a comprehensive picture of what is going on in the bush all over Australia. This means that governments often consult Frontier Services about what issues are important to people in the bush.

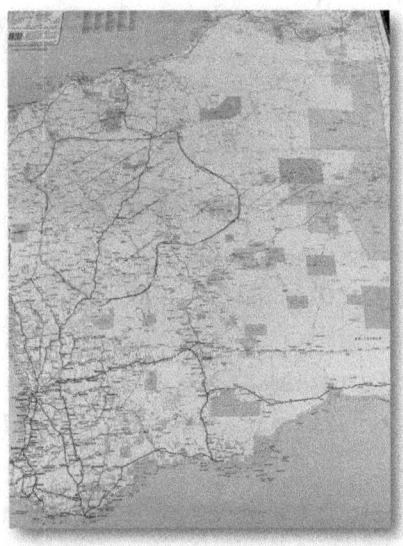

Part of Western Australia with Patrol Area (North)

First Impressions

Meekatharra is a pastoral and mining town, 800 kilometres south of Port Hedland and nearly 800 kilometres north east of Perth. In our time there our patrol comprised 157 stations, over 20 mines, a number of indigenous communities, and 6 small towns. Our patrol was about half the size of the state of South Australia.

Even before we got to Meekatharra, the experience was proving interesting. In 1985, much of the journey up from Perth was on single-width bitumen. This meant that when you saw a road train coming against you, the rule was to slow down and put two wheels off the bitumen. Many people went off at speed, causing the car to roll. It was our first insight into the benefits of taking things slowly. The weather was the second.

We knew it would be hot arriving in Meekatharra in January. However, knowing something and understanding it are two different things. After driving up, Bob turned around and flew commercially back to Perth to collect our Cessna 182. That first night, I made the decision not to sleep with the air conditioning on while he was away. My bright idea lasted about an hour. I hadn't realised that when the thermometer sits between the high-thirties and mid-forties day after day, you are lucky if the night-time temperatures drop below twenty-eight degrees. As it was pension night there was plenty of noise outside, but nothing could compete with the sound of our old air-conditioning unit.

Not long after we arrived, it rained. And it rained and it rained Twenty-three millilitres in twenty-four hours. We were relieved, as our empty tanks suddenly had enough water to meet our needs. Until we discovered that there was a leak in the pipe. The leak was quickly fixed, but that was the last of the rain until June 1986, a full eighteen months later, when we had ten inches.

One of the surprises in Meekatharra was the well-kept bougainvilleas planted in the middle of the main street. As with many of the early settled outback towns, the main street was wide, to allow enough room for the camel teams to turn around.

There were two supermarkets in the town – one very small Woolworths and another privately owned store, but to my dismay there was no hairdresser and no pharmacy. I did find a hairdresser working from home, and became a regular client of hers until she retired. Fortunately, her retirement coincided with the expansion of the privately owned supermarket, and they had added a hairdressing salon to their operation.

Signwriter, 1994

The trainers from the Pearce airfield often flew up to Meekatharra as an exercise. I heard them come in one day, as we happened to be at home, and Bob and I went out to meet them. On arriving, a Squadron Leader came to meet me, someone who I could not recall meeting before. He introduced himself, and said, "You won't remember me, but I came to your place for dinner." This was about 20 years before, when we invited young helicopter pilots in groups for dinner so that Bob could get to know them. He remembered what we had for entrée, main course, and dessert. He told me that one of my daughters, Mandi, had not enjoyed the cold soup, and nor did he. It was summer, so this was a new idea for soup. He then told me he had enjoyed all the rest of the meal.

CHAPTER 13
Life in The Murchison: Jenny

We were warned on arrival to be prepared that the seasons changed very abruptly. The change to winter wasn't so noticeable, and lasted a much shorter time than in Adelaide. During the cooler months, the station people became even busier than usual, doing the jobs that were too physically demanding in the very hot weather, such as shearing, mustering, well-sinking and fencing. From September, the thermometer would start to climb, first to the high twenties, and then creeping up into the thirties and gradually on into the forties.

The eighth of April 1992 proved to be an eventful day. We were relaxing at home when the house was engulfed in by very thick red dust storm. This was quickly followed by a loud bang on the roof of the manse, as though someone had thrown a rock. This was followed by another and then another. We went out on to the verandah to investigate, to discover that the house was being battered by hailstones.

A neighbour managed to store one of the hailstones in their freezer. On measuring it later, they found that it was seven inches—nearly eighteen centimetres—in diameter.

The dust storm had timed itself to coincide with school pick-up time, which was fortunate as all the children were able to get home before the hail began to hammer down onto the town. In fact, only two people were hurt during the storm— a man was hit on the shoulder by one of the huge stones, and a boy had his arm lacerated by broken glass when a hailstone smashed through a hopper window just as he was shutting it.

For us, the worst damage was to our little plane. We went to check it straight after the storm had passed, and were met by a very sad sight. The ailerons were damaged beyond repair, the flaps and elevators were badly dented, and the top surfaces looked as if someone had taken a hammer to them. The cost of repair totalled $17,500, which was fortunately covered by insurance—apart from the $1,000 excess. It was taken away for repairs to Perth, and we could not collect it until the middle of June, so in the interim we were restricted to operating as a driving patrol. As most roads were out of action, there was one occasion on which we needed to hire a plane in order to attend a very important double baptism.

Bob & Jenny with Plane

Damage across the town was substantial. Only one solar panel escaped unscathed, while every asbestos roof developed leaks, causing water damage to the properties they had provided shelter to. It took months, and in some cases years, for the cars to have their windshields and bodywork repaired. Two brand-new cars had been purchased less than a week before the storm, and although one of the dealers kindly replaced the damaged vehicle, the other one was sent for repairs. Our car and the patrol car were under the carport but not fully covered, and our car suffered a broken windscreen from a ricocheting hailstone. Two windowpanes in the church and one in the Lowan Centre were broken—Bob quickly repaired all these windows with new glass. A large tree in the garden was uprooted, although we fortunately managed to prop it up with a block and tackle so that it continued to grow. The very worst damage in town was to the Catholic Church. The building had an asbestos roof which was extensively damaged, resulting in much of the plaster from the ceiling falling onto the wooden pews and damaging everything inside the church. It took four months to fully repair the church.

The hailstorm had hit a station 200 miles to the west before travelling to Meekatharra, and then moving on to a second station 200 miles to the east. No damage was found in between each of these three spots, so of all the places that the storm chose to let rip before moving on, it chose the ones where it would do the most damage. Fortunately, the two stations got off comparatively lightly.

Work Parties
In August 1986, the first work party came to Meekatharra, from Stawell in Victoria. The work party had been arranged by the UCA, who had written the year before, to say they were planning on taking two coach loads of their members on

tour across the Nullarbor and thence to Meekatharra, before travelling on along the Gunbarrell Highway. They asked what work we would like done, and we had sent what we felt was an impossibly long list, expecting them to tell us what they would be able to tackle, so that we could have the appropriate materials ready for them.

The jobs included replacing the front fence, painting the church, and lining the Lowan Centre, which was a shed that we used for Sunday School and overflow accommodation. They said that they could do all the jobs, if we provided the materials. At 7 pm on the 29th of August, a crowd of people ranging in age from fifteen to eighty arrived on two forty-six seater coaches.

This wonderful group not only carried out all the jobs on the list we had sent through, they also made much-needed new curtains for the church, fixed a problem in the roof, made handrails for the back steps of the church, and tidied the garden full of native plants. We had a great deal of fun while the work party was there, and all jobs were finished by Saturday night.

Everyone camped at the high school, but all the cooking was done from a trailer parked outside the manse, and on Saturday night we had a wonderful concert. After church on Sunday we arranged a barbecue for the work party and the locals, and everyone had a great time. They set off early the following morning to travel the Gunbarrell Highway. We had two letters soon after, from each coach-load of people—one saying they'd had a very uneventful trip, and the other saying they got bogged in sand and had to push start the bus! Both groups added that Meeka was the very best part of the trip. Many saw their trip as a good holiday. We saw it as a miracle.

A month or two later, one of our Aboriginal families was burnt out. Although they sadly lost their home and most of their possessions, they luckily all escaped with their lives. It was good to be able to offer them the Lowan Centre until Homes West could offer then another home, and the town rallied round to help them. While they were in the Lowan Centre we moved the Sunday School onto our manse verandah, and used the spare bedrooms in the manse for overflow accommodation.

Not long after this, some visitors from Perth arrived. When I told them about the work party, they were very keen to offer their help. As we'd just had all our major repairs carried out, I suggested that Mount Magnet might appreciate their help, as it was the only other place we had our own UCA Church.

Mount Magnet Church Before Work Party

Within a matter of days, three people travelled up from Perth to look at the situation. At the time we had pigeons living in the church, which meant a big cleaning job each time we used the

Church. As well as dealing with the pigeons, the church also needed painting and new curtains. As the small group went round inspecting everything, I explained that I didn't think we would have enough money to fix everything. One man looked at me and asked, "Why do you think I am here?" I knew one of the men was a builder and the other was a painter, so my reply was that I didn't know. He replied, "I am a financier, so you don't need to worry about the money."

A few weeks after their visit, a work party came up and really thrilled the town when, after doing all our jobs, they had some paint left over, which they used to paint the CWA house next door.

After the work party had put wire up to stop the pigeons getting in, we only had to contend with the Singapore ants, which would appear the moment you stood still. They could give a good bite, and so everyone would shuffle from foot to foot when talking to people.

More Weather
In June 1989, three-and-a-half inches of rain fell over much of the Murchison. Green grass and herbage replaced the dusty red of the outback, with smiles abounding. Some stations lost sheep and fences were damaged, so that shearing was delayed for some. We had roads closed and many of the strips were too soft to land on, but no-one was complaining about rain. Not all our stations received this welcome rain in 1989, but the following summer the heavy rains fell in abundance, which set the area up for quite a few years, which was a great relief as several years of drought followed these good rains.

That summer in the Murchison was a time of great contrasts. The expectation was that summer was relentlessly hot. That year, it was very hot until the middle of January, and then the storms rolled in and the days became remarkably cool. February 1990 was the coolest on record, with not a single day over forty degrees for the whole month. March returned to the usual pattern of summer, with almost every day hitting forty, but by then most of the Murchison had rain—even areas that had been in drought for many years. It was wonderful to see green grass and fat stock. The downside was that the rains also brought lots of mosquitoes and more flies than usual, although there were always plenty of flies, so it didn't make too much difference. There was also a great increase in the number of kangaroos and feral goats.

This cool, wet summer was far from the norm, and during the years that we were there it was distressing to see the prospect of a good season fading rapidly as the temperatures soared, knowing how hard times would be if the rain didn't come. However, these wonderful people stayed cheerful, saying that it was no good worrying about the weather as they couldn't do anything about it. However, in spite of being philosophical about the weather, when the heat was relentless they always worried about their animals.

The weather during the summer in the outback requires keeping a watchful eye whilst flying. December temperatures can vary from thirty-seven degrees to well over forty. One December the thermometer hit forty every single day. Flying in those conditions, it becomes important to keep a very careful eye out for the build up of thunderstorms, willy willies, and lightening. Lightening and small aeroplanes do not mix, and I always handed over to Bob when there was any danger of lightening. High temperatures also meant increased turbulence, with a much more frequent occurrence of being lifted up or down by strong winds. As the weather cools, there are fewer potholes in the sky, and the aircraft performs far better.

Captain Speaking

On one occasion when I was flying, I was caught in a sheer downdraft. This is when a very strong wind is pushing the plane down even when the pilot is trying to climb, and with the engine going as fast as possible. Being inexperienced, as the ground drew nearer and nearer I became increasingly worried that I would not be able to stop us from crashing, so I asked Bob to come on as well. His only response was a mischievous grin. I had no choice but to hold on tight. Just as I thought all hope was lost, I felt the plane starting to rise. Bob knew we would run into ground effect and stop descending.

One summer we travelled to the west—to the Murchison Shire—with our daughter, Fiona, her husband, Peter, their three small children, and their house girl, Riko, from the Solomon Islands. Peter, Riko, and the children flew over with Bob in the plane, while Fiona and I made our way in the Urvan. It was the Saturday before Christmas, and the big event was a cricket match, which was to be followed by a meal, then the arrival of Father Christmas and finally carol singing in the evening. As Murchison Shire was the only shire in Australia without a town, and with a grand total of twenty-three ratepayers, there was no hotel. We needed to stay overnight, and so the plan was for some of us to sleep in the Urvan, while the rest of us slept either under the wing of the plane or the verandah of the small museum.

The cricket match went off without a hitch, but as we were about to have a meal the rain arrived! This was most unexpected! There was no way anyone was going to be able to sleep under the wing of the plane, and so after some rather damp carol singing Bob and I slept on the verandah, and the others all squashed up together in the Urvan.

Early the next morning I drove the Urvan over the strip, to make sure the plane would not get bogged taking off. Bob then left with his planeload of people, and Fiona and I drove home. I worried that we had to cross the Murchison River, which at that time did not have a bridge crossing, and that the rains may have caused flooding. However, my fears were unfounded. Although the unmade road at the start of the drive was very boggy, we soon ran out of wet road and were then blowing red dust behind us. When we reached Mullewa, instead of travelling south we turned east towards Mount Magnet, driving straight into a strong wind which the Urvan did not particularly like. On reaching Mount Magnet I stopped to fill up with petrol, while Fiona called Bob to let him know that it was taking us longer than expected to get home due to the strong winds. She asked if he was flying to Sandstone for a church service, only to be told he was at home because Meekatharra was on red alert for a cyclone. I really wasn't thrilled about the idea of driving straight into a cyclone, but all went well and we arrived home before it reached us.

Gold

The price of gold is always very carefully watched. During our time in Meeka it fluctuated from quite low to high. When it went up, one of the mines built houses for their workers instead of having them 'fly-in-fly-out', which brought the population up to about 1,600, making Meekatharra a flourishing town.

Meekatharra has always been primarily a pastoral town, with the addition of intermittent mining. At one stage, Meeka was the rail head from Perth. Now, there is no railway travelling further north of Perth than Geraldton. Due to all the growth years after the price of gold increased, we had a beautiful new motel, a second butcher, a remodelled supermarket, a lovely sporting complex, and a second TV channel. But all progress comes at a cost—we also had six 'stop' signs, almost as many 'give way' signs, and we often had to park a full thirty metres from the shop! We even had to look both ways before we crossed the road. Before the gold boom the shops used close for an hour or two for lunch, after the gold boom they opened at 8.30 am and stayed open till 5.30 pm—even on Saturdays.

Here Comes The Sun

Stations started getting solar power whilst we were in the patrol. One of the first stations to begin using solar power on a large scale had been using a small solar set up for some time—just enough to run the TV or a small appliance. They upgraded this to a twenty-four volt system with large storage capacity and a modern electronic inverter. This provided enough power to run an electric freezer, a refrigerator, the house lights, and the TV.

More Weather, And Economic Woes

In 1991 we had been having a good season over most of the patrol, but with a very-low wool price and an alarming drop in the gold price, shivers of apprehension were around. The high Australian dollar made the situation worse. Some small mines closed, and some stations were fearful but managed to hang on.

By the end of the year, the wool growers were hurting. The high cost of fuel had hit everyone, but the ones who were hurting the most were the wool growers in the pastoral areas. They had no way of diversifying and had to keep growing wool, but the reduction in wool prices combined with the 30% tax on all wool sold meant their income was slashed in half. There was talk of a 70% quota, which would have cut incomes by a further 30%. Very few could have survived that. Part of the problem was overproduction, but that was not the fault of the pastoralists—it was caused by farmers going into wool to profit from the high prices which were on offer two years before.

The downturn in the Eastern European, Russian, and Chinese economies added to the problems, and we were finding a good deal of anger and bewilderment as we visited the stations. High interest rates of 20% or more did not help, and some properties were already up for sale.

By September 1991 the worries were turning around. The weather was at its best with blue skies, moderate temperatures, and light winds. Most areas had had enough rain to fatten stock from the bad days of the drought, though most areas needed more rain to see them through the long hot summer. The slow upturn of wool prices had improved seasonal prospects. We started to see a few smiles on our travels.

Even so, there was still uneasiness amongst the pastoralists, as the tenure of pastoral leases was under threat. There was concern that Aboriginal land rights would cause huge problems, and gossip was rife. Frontier Services kept us up to date on the facts of what would happen, and we were able to reassure the pastoralists that they really did not have major worries. The other concern was the new Pastoral Tenure Act which was before the State Parliament. One of the provisions said that Aboriginal people would be given unrestricted access to pastoral leases at any time without the need to seek permission from the leaseholder. The pastoralists' worry was that large bands of Aboriginal people would interfere with mustering and the management of the lands, leaving gates open and frightening stock away from watering point. However, most pastoralists had a good relationship with local Aboriginals, and we felt they were being stirred up by extremists not living in the area. Once again, we offered as much reassurance as we could, and with time, the pastoralists came to see that their fears were groundless.

The last part of 1991 brought drought as well as the recession, so some men worked in the mines or went cutting sandalwood, leaving their wives, who already had a very heavy workload, to look after the few remaining stock for the days they were away. Some were trying to sell before their debts exceeded the value of their stations, which was a difficult task in a time of drought.

June 1992 brought the breaking of the drought for the whole of the patrol area. We had at least eight inches across the area, and some parts had twice that amount. The desert area became lush, and the wildflowers were incredible, with huge swathes of white, pink or yellow flowers sitting alongside each other.

The only downside was that the breaking of the drought brought cooler weather, and so we were all complaining about how cold it was!

Remote Work
As Bob knew a number of Vietnam veterans, he had been adopted by the Pilbara Region Veterans as a sort of unofficial chaplain for their association. He felt honoured to be invited to conduct a memorial service at Tom Price on the anniversary of the Battle of Long Tan—a battle he had been involved in.

Not long after this, Bob was invited to visit Mungilli—one of the most remote Aboriginal camps in Australia. About 50 people had made a settlement there, in an effort to get away from the drunkenness and problems they were encountering in the wider community, and also to protect some important tribal sites which had suffered at the hands of mining companies. One had been almost completely destroyed with explosives. They had done a lot to make the settlement viable, but the lack of health services and school, combined with a 1,200 kilometre round trip for supplies each week made the task to difficult. As a result, after some time most of the people left.

Action!

Bob was Chair of the Meekatharra Community Action Group. This was formed to look at building a hostel for people with a disability, as well as for the aged. We already had a home care service up and running, but the community action group secured a grant of $1million, which enabled us to build a small hostel near the hospital, with six bedrooms complete with ensuite, and a verandah. The verandah was very important, as most aboriginal people wanted to sleep outside, though not all residents were aboriginal.

At the same time, a separate community centre with a kitchen was added, and finally a day centre completed the complex. It was a very worthwhile project.

Our involvement in that project, along with the CWA, the Meekatharra Land Conservation Committee, the Isolated Children's Parents' Association, Girl Guides, and Presbytery helped to keep us busy—along with our visits to the stations, mines, towns, and aboriginal communities

Daycare Opening, 1992

CHAPTER 14
The Annual Cricket Match: Bob

The 26th January dawned fine and hot, and I prepared my first flight plan with great care. Paroo is only sixty-seven nautical miles by air from Meekatharra, so I did not expect to have any trouble finding it. To my chagrin, I missed the station and had to do a bit of a square search. The homestead is surrounded by trees, which makes it quite hard to see, but we finally found it and landed on the large strip about a mile from the station. A vehicle came out and picked us up. In later years we always used the small strip next to the homestead, but it looked a bit small to my inexperienced eye.

The ground behind the homestead had been marked out for the cricket, with a white line drawn on the hard-baked red earth. There was a concrete pitch covered with a very decrepit old coir mat, and a large gidgee tree in the field of play. I was asked if I would be playing. "Not if I can get out of it!" I said. This was taken to mean, "Yes please!" so I found myself in the 'townies' team.

It was blazingly hot. Fortunately, as there were nineteen players on each team and only eleven allowed to field at any one time, there was some respite. I made five runs and bowled several overs without success, but despite that, our side won. After the match we repaired to the shade and met many of the folk we would be visiting over the next nine years. It was simply amazing how quickly we were accepted as a part of the community. It says a lot about the quality of the ministry of previous patrol padres that it was assumed we would fit in.

The afternoon ended with a sheaf tossing competition, and then we had a barbecue for dinner with neighbours bringing salads and desserts. An Anglican minister and I conducted a short ecumenical service in the small chapel near the house and beer flowed freely until bedtime. Everyone who was staying the night, which was more than half the visitors, slept on shearer's beds or on swags on the lawn until first light—the flies made sure that no one had a lie-in!

We had the opportunity to continue to get to know many of the people in our new community over a hearty breakfast of mutton chops, eggs, bacon and toast, all washed down with strong tea, before flying home again, very well-satisfied with our reception into the community of the Murchison area.

CHAPTER 15

Women: Jenny

It is an interesting and busy life on a station. Women do not see other women very often. As most of the stations were still on the Royal Flying Doctor radio when we first arrived in Meekatharra, your news would travel over a wide area. Although there were advantages to these 'galah' sessions, the downside was that it was impossible to hold a private conversation with a doctor or a family member. However, the radio schedules did give women contact with other women, and also helped each designated RFDS area to become an integrated community

Picture coming back with your first baby onto a station of a million acres, with your nearest neighbour at least sixty kilometres away by road. With the radio sessions, if you have a bad night with your new baby and are worried that there is something wrong, you can ring someone and get advice, from anyone listening in, rather than just one-to-one advice, which is what happened when the telephones came in.

As a result of this exclusion from the radio service, incorporating new people into such a widespread community became much more difficult with the introduction of telephones, in spite of the advantages of being able to have a private conversation.

Networking
As the telephones proved to be problematic, I applied for and was given a grant by the Western Australian State Government to study networking for women in the outback. What had

prompted me to apply was our perception that the sense of community, which had been so strong when we arrived, had rapidly decreased to worrying levels since the arrival of telephones in the outback.

With the Flying Doctor Radio, everyone knew all the good and bad news in the community and supported each other. With the advent of the telephone, new people were not easily assimilated into the community, and everyone had become more isolated. Additionally, as people were not used to timed calls, when the first bills came in they were enormous, as most people lived in different zones. After this, husbands told their wives not to use the telephone unless it was an emergency, which added to the women's isolation. I wanted to see what was being done in other states, as most of them had been using telephones for a while. I also looked at overseas areas, such as northern Canada, and Finland where people were cut off for a time throughout the winter (but they were all living in communities, rather than single families units).

In order to gather all the data I needed, I visited Alice Springs, Katherine, Darwin, Mount Isa, Sydney, Wagga Wagga, Melbourne, and Port Augusta. It sounds like a funny collection of places, but in some cases an outback service was being run from the centre in a city location. There were also individuals in these cities who were able to offer me important insights. In Sydney, I met the head of an organisation that sent helpers out to stations, and in Melbourne I went to see Telstra—or Telecom as it was at the time. My idea was that women could pick five other women they wanted to have as 'untimed call' contacts. My first question to Telecom was to ask if this was technically possible. The answer came back very brightly, "Oh yes."

I then outlined my plan. Their faces fell. "Oh no, they might block the lines."

I assured them that during the first month this might be a possibility, but once the novelty wore off, the level of usage would drop down, as they were very busy people and mostly did not have time for long chats. After three weeks of discussions, I arrived home with mountains of material to sort out.

Once I had sorted through everything, I made three recommendations. Only one came to fruition. I recommended a quarterly magazine run by station people, and a remote family area service, and the 'untimed call' contacts list. The UCA looked at the remote family area service recommendation very carefully, but felt that if they started it in one area, there would soon be requests to expand and the cost would be too great.

The telephone hook up also did not come to fruition. However, the quarterly magazine was taken up. We secured a grant for a computer, a printer and five fax machines. The reason for the latter was that we had five editors all feeding information and ideas over the widespread country. We called the newsletter *Bush Voices*, and it meant that even if it was a little late, everyone heard all the news.

Marriage, Kids, And Extra Mouths

Some newly married woman had come from other stations, but there were those who had come from a city, and met their future husbands when they were working as a jillaroo on a station.

For the women who had come from a city, living on a station was a completely different life. For instance, when it came to shearing time, there would be a huge influx of people on the station, rather than just the husband and wife. Although there were shearers' quarters with cooking facilities—and their own cook— there had to be extra hands for mustering, at which point it became the wife's job to cook for all the musters. The same applied to the cattle stations, as there would be musters to look after.

Years ago, most stations had a governesses for the children, and a cook for the family and the shearers and musters. By the time we joined the patrol, the stations usually only had a husband or wife, sometimes with the addition of the husband or wife's parents.

Women became very good a coping with having extra mouths to feed, but once the children arrived it could become a complicated juggling act—looking after the musters, looking after the children, taking on the role of teacher as well as mum, as the children only had half an hour a day with the School of the Air teacher. It was a busy life! For this reason, we stayed away from the stations during shearing or mustering, unless we were specifically asked to be there.

Birth

On a visit to a station not long after we joined the patrol, we found that a new mum, who had travelled the 600 kilometres to Geraldton to see a gynaecologist, had received no advice about preparing for the birth. When she asked about what to expect, the gynaecologist simply patted her on the shoulder and said, "Don't worry, we will look after you."

Not very reassuring when that gynaecologist is a 600 kilometre drive from where you plan to have your baby.

On hearing this, we went to Perth and asked the Department of Health if they could send us some relevant material to help women on stations prepare for births. The upshot was they created a book, a video, a relaxation programme, and a course of antenatal exercises. We also had a physiotherapist with particular interest in antenatal exercises come up to Meekatharra with us to talk to several pregnant women. The people on the stations were very happy to receive the same sort of help as the city people.

Raising The Next Generation
During the time that I was looking into networking for women in the outback, Bob was working on community initiatives of his own. His idea was to travel to a number of remote Aboriginal communities and ask what education services they would like for their children. Unfortunately, the trip turned out to be very hard.

The government sent two people to accompany him. Bob explained to these government employees that he would ask the men and women what they wanted for their children, and then everyone would sit in silence for at least an hour. He said that although it might appear as though nothing was happening during this period of silence, in fact a lot of thought would be going into what was going to be needed. After everything had been carefully considered, then they would be ready to talk.

It was agreed that Bob would ask the question, and then they would all settle down to wait.

They arrived at the Aboriginal community and sat down with everyone. Bob asked the question about what they felt they wanted for their children's education. After less than a minute's silence, one of the government employees jumped in, saying, "Would you like a playgroup?" They had no idea what a playgroup was, but replied that they would try it.

This pattern was repeated and repeated, until finally, after three days, Bob met a nurse who had been with the community for years. She said, "I know what they want. They want their children to be able to read and write and have enough arithmetic to work in the store."

And so that was what Bob reported.

In the nine years we were in Meekatharra I was constantly impressed with all the women in the small towns and on the stations, as well as the Aboriginal mothers and grandmothers, who worked hard to bring their children up to attend school. Not always through to Year 12, but still to a good standard of education—which was much harder for small, isolated communities.

The Country Women's Association Art Exhibitions
Near the end of 1989, a woman from a nearby station was telling me that she had done an art course by correspondence a few years earlier, but hadn't had the opportunity to paint for some time, owing to her mother's long illness. As her mother had recently died, I thought that picking up her paint brush again may prove to be a welcome pursuit, and so I floated the idea with her that, subject to their agreement, the Meekatharra Country Women's Association (CWA) might hold an exhibition of her work. Little did I know what this casual remark would lead to!

The CWA were very keen on the idea. However, the small,

solo artist exhibition that I'd initially had in mind was not shared by the rest of the community. When word spread, the suggestions poured in. Had we thought of inviting this or that artist to participate? Would we hire the recreation centre? How would we find a time of the year that suited everyone? How could we involve the Aboriginal community? The suggestions were so numerous that we soon knew we would not be able to please everyone.

Nevertheless, we hoped that the full-scale art exhibition that we had planned for the 25th and 26th of August 1990 would please most of the people. The intention was that it would be a one-off event—just as the intention had been to have a small, solo artist exhibition. It was never planned as a fundraiser, but purely as a way of encouraging and promoting local artists. We picked the new sports complex as the venue, as it was modern, with good lighting, and not too big. Altogether we had five artists, one of whom was an experienced Aboriginal craftswoman. She exhibited a range of work, including woodwork and carved emu eggs— with pride of place going to a copy of an emu egg that she had carved for the queen. The other four artists were all from stations. At the last minute we got a fifth station woman who was a potter. None of the station women had exhibited before. We encouraged them to frame all their paintings and told them not to put too low a value on their work. Then we got down to the detailed organising everything.

Each artist gave us a list of people they wanted to attend the private view and we sent out the invitations. We bought cheese and wine, just as if it were an opening in the city. We borrowed screens to hang the paintings, arranged extra lighting, designed and printed a catalogue, bought red spot stickers to put on the paintings as they sold, and spent all day arranging the paintings to the best effect. Then we held our breath. In the end, the only real mistake we made was being too successful. We invited about 130 people, including quite a few from Perth and Geraldton, and anticipated that about 60 would come. However, almost everyone who was invited came! By the end of the evening, most of the paintings had red dots on them. The next day, when the exhibition opened to the general public, people who had not been invited to the opening were very upset that the paintings they wanted to buy had already been sold.

As a result of this exhibition, three of the artists were invited to exhibit in Perth, where they once again sold almost everything they showed.

Much to my surprise people started asking when next year's exhibition would be taking place, and enquiring as to whether we could include crafts as well. For the following four years the CWA continued to hold an art-and-craft exhibition, with each one becoming bigger and more popular than its predecessor. In fact, after the first year we moved to the much bigger Shire Hall in Meekatharra. The fourth exhibition coincided with Meekatharra's centenary and was the biggest to date. Much to everyone's delight, there was a competition for the artists with $1,000 prize money.

Moving the exhibition to the Shire Hall meant reorganising everything. The lighting in the hall was not sufficient to show off the paintings, and we needed more screens to display the artwork. Each year we found new artists to join the previous year's exhibitors. After the first year, the artists received more support from their families, as they had discovered how much the paintings were prized. This gave our artists more confidence to experiment with new ideas. Alongside the artists, the exhibitions involved a wide number of members of the community. For instance, one company lent us some floodlights and helped to install them, while the school and hospital lent us screens to display the paintings.

After the first exhibition there was no private view, and the opening instead became was a public event, with tickets available both before the night and on the door. The organisers would be there for most of the day, getting everything ready. For the first three years, Bob hung all the paintings, whilst I checked in the exhibits and others set up tables for the craft and organised the food and wine.

The second year, the exhibition was due to open at 7 pm, with sales starting at 7.45 pm. By 6.30 pm there was a queue waiting at the door. One of our artists actually wanted to buy one of her own paintings as a gift for someone. She was third in the queue, and was disappointed to find it had already been sold while she was waiting.

From the second year onwards we had a visiting guest artist to open the exhibitions, and each year the guest artist was astounded by the high-standard of art that had been produced. We had a variety of drawing and paintings in mediums including pen and ink, pencil, watercolour, oil, acrylic, pastel, and charcoal, along with a very interesting photography section. As the number of local artists taking part grew we had to limit the amount of entries they could put in to fifteen, with a maximum of one not for sale. The guest artist was allowed eight paintings only. One of our guest artists remarked to Bob that she had never seen an art show so well lit and hung. The opening night became a social gathering not to be missed.

As well as talented artists, we had some exceptional craftspeople. One of our members came up with new ideas for her beautiful pottery every year, and found it hard to keep up a supply of pottery in between the exhibitions. All the craft generated a great deal of interest, from the cottage crafts to the ceramics to the quilts, and the artefacts produced by the Aboriginals from Wiluna.

A New Home
In 1989, much to my surprise, I found myself taking the role of president of the Meekatharra Branch of the CWA. I began my presidency not long after the branch had decided that the rooms we used were no longer suitable for our activities. Throughout the 1980's the number of members had dropped down to six, but as the effects of the mining boom started to be felt in Meekatharra, there were more young women in town with no family support. As a result, the CWA became a focal point for social activities. There was a need for somewhere safe in the building for preschool children to play while their mothers were using the centre. On top of this, some of the CWA members were running an opportunity shop one day a week. It was highly successful, but very hard to run in the old building. All in all, making the decision that we needed a new building was easy. The hard part was going to be raising the funds.

The original building had been purchased in 1946 for the princely sum of ninety-five pounds ($190). Before becoming the CWA headquarters, it had been a miner's cottage. This meant that the framework had been put up for two rooms and a small kitchen, with a verandah wrapping around two-and-a-half sides of the building, enclosed up to waist height, and then with latticework for the top half. As it had been expensive to bring up sheeting from Perth over dirt roads at the time the cottage was been built, where there was a verandah, the walls were lined on the inside only.

Old CWA House

The interior consisted of one fairly large room, a small bedroom, a small kitchen, and a toilet off the verandah. In the backyard was a ramshackle, galvanised iron shed, which had once been the bathroom, although by the time the CWA took possession, it had become unusable. Because inland air is so dry, the timber in the houses in the Murchison dries out and becomes cracked and brittle. Eventually, it will no longer hold a nail. This makes repairs very difficult and very expensive. That was the stage the old CWA house had reached. In any case, it was too small and lacked the basic facilities.

As the membership grew, so did our determination to get better accommodation. Just before I became president, the decision was taken to run a fete. As plans were progressing, the serving president and her family had to move away from Meekatharra, and I suddenly found myself elevated from vice-president to the top spot.

Everyone worked very hard on organising the fete for six months, until finally the day dawned bright and clear. Soon, everyone was up at the sporting complex and on the oval putting up tents and setting out their stalls. We had arranged for the children's television character Fat Cat to come from Geraldton with the television crew to open the fete. The day proved a great success—more so for us than Fat Cat. Although the day was not hot, it was warm enough—in the mid-thirties—and so the poor girl inside the Fat Cat costume, who had thought she would only be waving a hanky to open the fete, had to hide in a small room and remove the top half of the costume to cool down for a few minutes, before heading back out to meet and greet Fat Cat's adoring public. In the end, the fete was well worth all the planning and effort, and Fat Cat's discomfort, as we raised close to $5,000 that day. This gave a boost to our hopes of a new building, so we decided that we would continue with our fundraising, in the hopes of affording a transportable house.

With our op shop increasing in popularity, and the 10%

commission we took for our art and craft exhibitions, our finances grew. We had a badge-making machine that proved popular, and ran fashion parades— including one for children— along with raffles, lamington drives, and further annual fetes. At the end of two-and-a-half years we had $30,000, including some donations from other branches.

In 1991, we had the opportunity to purchase a nearly new three-bedroom air-conditioned transportable house with a double carport, a pergola, a clothes hoist, and even some fencing. All of this was delivered, and the house set up on site for $46,000. Headquarters in Perth had been interested in our growing savings, and had given us a $10,000 grant, plus a $15,000 interest-free loan. Coupled with a second interest-free loan of $5,000 from another branch, we were able to demolish the old building, purchase and install the transportable, and install a new leach drain. The latter is not a cheap exercise, as the ground is so hard that gelignite has to be used.

All this happened in August, just as we were finalising our big first art-and-craft exhibition in the Shire Hall. The telephone was ringing constantly, and it felt as though our small group had over-committed. However, by November, it was a very proud branch that hosted the opening of the new house, with Mrs Dinnie, the State President of CWA, performing the opening ceremony, and Mrs Alice Campbell, who had been behind the purchase of the first house in 1946, attending. The following day, an ecumenical service was held in the town, attended by many of our visitors as well as local people. Bob and Father Bert, the Catholic priest, ran the service, which was very deeply appreciated by all who came.

New CWA House

The community supported all our fundraising ventures, with the Lions Club even putting up the carport and the pergola for us. Just over two years after the opening, the hard work of the members ensured that the two loans had been paid back. The important thing about the new building was that we could use it for so many things. The op shop continued to grow, and to be an important part of life in Meekatharra. The house could now be used for craft classes, book reviews, and mahjong. Many functions were held in it, and station people were able to use the house to stay overnight when visiting the doctor, or coming in for gymkhanas, weddings and other events.

The members were a forward-thinking group, interested in making the branch both active and suitable for the needs of people living in the area, as well as showing an interest in wider community concerns. We had members attending both divisional meetings and the State Conference. It was a great branch of which to be a member.

Distances

The tyranny of distance made it very difficult for our division of the CWA to meet. It was therefore arranged to have an annual general meeting once a year and, when possible, a rally. The latter often depended on the weather, as well as shearing and mustering times. Early in our first year in the Murchison, Mount Magnet was to hold the AGM. As we owned a Nissan Urvan, which could carry nine people, I offered to drive the two-hundred kilometres to Mount Magnet, in order to save two cars having to make the trip. We only had six members back then, but much to my surprise, the seats of the Urvan were very quickly filled by the members of our branch and several members of the Wiluna branch.

The reason for my surprise was that none of the women had driven with me before, and that particular road, though sealed, was only one lane wide, and heavily used by road trains, cattle, sheep, emus and kangaroos. With such a road, it is very easy to roll over if the car is driven onto the dirt, and so I thought some of the women might be nervous driving with me.

However, in the end the journey was fine and it proved a very good day—although longer than we had expected, which meant travelling home after dark, when the worry is hitting a kangaroo. One husband rang Bob, very concerned about where we were. Bob decided to drive down to look for us. As he started out I was in Meekatharra, dropping some of my passengers back home. This meant that he travelled about a hundred kilometres without finding us. It was a lesson to me to ring before setting out on the return journey, which would have saved us all a lot of worry.

In April 1992, when Meekatharra held the AGM in our lovely new house, one of our members suggested that we bless the house. This was a custom she had known and liked before she migrated from Italy. We all liked the idea, and so Bob blessed the house. We hope that it will always shelter people and be a happy place.

One year, our AGM was held at Murchison Shire, now known as Murchison Settlement. It is the only shire in Australia without a town. The shortest way there is approximately 400 kilometres from Meekatharra, with only 80 kilometres of that on sealed road, and the journey was anticipated to be very rough due to heavy rain. Once again, I said that I would take the Urvan. This proved to be a popular offer, with two women driving over 100 kilometres to reach me before we set out.

We arranged to drive down, stay the night at a nearby station, go to the meeting, and then drive home. This meant driving home part of the way at night. Rather facetiously, I commented that we could expect to get one flat tyre and hit a kangaroo. I must have known something, as we punctured one tyre on the way over and were hit by a kangaroo on the way back. It was more of an inconvenience than anything, as we always carried two spare tyres, along with plenty of water. In spite of the somewhat difficult journey, it was well worth the trip. There were about twenty-five women at the meeting, and we all enjoyed catching up, especially with seldom-seen friends. On the way home one person remarked, "Weren't we lucky to spend so long with so many women!"

CHAPTER 16

Children: Jenny

A station owner had just moved to a new homestead. He and his five-year-old son had travelled to the boy's grandparents' home in a country town about 700 kilometres away, in order to pick up some items they had stored there during the move. They were getting ready to leave when the boy pointed to a standard lamp.

"Dad, we're taking this lamp, aren't we?"

"No, we're not taking the lamp. That belongs to your grandparents," his father replied.

The boy was silent for a moment, before making a second attempt. "We really need to take that lamp, Dad."

"Why?" His father asked, puzzled by his son's insistence.

"Because it works even when the generator isn't on," came the boy's simple response.

On the station, if he couldn't hear the sound of the generator, he knew that meant there was no electricity to power the lights.

Danger

It is easy for children to get lost if they wander away from the homestead. To prevent this from happening, some parents ensure their young children are barefoot. The reason is that the abundance of sharp prickles in the bush ensure that the children have no inclination to walk very far without shoes. If, as is usual, the homestead yard is kept free of these prickles, and the child strays out of the yard, their cries will soon attract their parents' attention. A further discouragement in the summer is that the ground becomes too hot for tender young feet.

What is amazing is that by the time children reach four or five years' old, they are able to walk barefoot over the hot ground and the prickles. Consequently, they have to know what to do if they go too far from home. Once out of sight of the homestead, it is easy to become disorientated. Bush children often quickly adapt and develop an extremely good sense of direction, learning to navigate using the sun and the stars. However, there are exceptions!

One afternoon, a nine-year-old girl went for a walk. After walking for a while, she realised that she was bushed. Her dad had let her know what to do if she ever got lost—find a track and follow it, as it would lead to a homestead or a fence. He'd told her that every paddock has at least two windmills, usually at the corners, and that she should follow the fence line until she came to a windmill. Once she reached the windmill, she should stay there and wait to be found. And so this is what she did. It was getting dark by the time she reached the windmill in the corner of the paddock, so she had a drink of water from the tank and settled down for the night. In the morning, she was able to recognise where she was, and set off for home. She'd nearly made it all the way back when the search party found her.

This is the minimum level of bushcraft that parents need to teach their children.

Driving

Bush children are not only self-reliant on foot. Children from around six years old will all have their own motorbike, of a suitable size. They also learn to drive cars and other vehicles early. Most station tracks are private roads, and so the children can learn legally, away from the public highway. Our first experience with a young driver came one morning when we landed on a station strip about two kilometres from the homestead. As we taxied up to the end of the strip, a Nissan patrol vehicle pulled up. Neither of us could see the driver. The door swung open, and a seven-year-old boy clambered out of the driver's seat. We piled in, and he started the engine, sliding down in the seat to let the clutch in, and pulling himself up with the steering wheel to let the clutch engage. Once we were moving, he could just touch the accelerator with the tips of his toes, but he couldn't see over the dashboard without pulling himself up on the wheel. As we gathered speed, he announced that he needed to change gear. As he slid down to let the clutch in, Bob reached for the steering wheel, only to think better of it when the boy fixed him with an icy glare.

When he was up and holding the wheel again he said, "I think we'll stay in that gear." He drove us very safely all the way to the homestead, including the tricky creek crossing, which he navigated with the confidence of a seasoned professional.

A few weeks after this experience we were met at another strip by another miniature chauffeur, of a similar age. He drove a smaller vehicle—a Suzuki. As he was taking us to the homestead he asked very nonchalantly, "Who is the youngest person to drive you around?" We told him about our drive in the Nissan and told him the age of the other boy. In a very disappointed voice, he confessed that the other boy was three weeks younger than him!

On another occasion we were met by two young brothers on suitably small motorbikes. Both boys dinked us back to the homestead over the roughest parts of the ground they could find!

Generally speaking, the boys start driving cars around the station at seven and the girls at about nine. This is simply because the girls often have to wait a little longer in order to have the physical strength to steer the vehicles. By the time these young people reach an age where they can be tested for their driver's licence they are excellent bush drivers, and can manage cars and trucks in all sorts of situations.

An example of their prowess is the story of an eleven-year-old girl. One afternoon, when her father and brothers were out on the run, she noticed that one of their dogs had an injured foot. Her mother bent down to see what was wrong, and when she was examining the paw, she touched the tender spot and the dog sprang up and bit her across the bridge of the nose. Within seconds, her eyes had become so swollen that she couldn't see. Her daughter helped her into their car and then drove over a hundred kilometres to the hospital in Meekatharra. This journey comprised almost entirely of dirt roads, with just a short distance on the main sealed road at the end of the journey. Once in town, she drove past the police station and pulled up outside the hospital. Two hours later, once the mother had been treated, they headed back home. The mother drove them to the edge of the town, but her eyes were still swollen and driving was a strain, so once they reached the dirt road the little girl took over and drove the rest of the way home. The mother was grateful but not particularly impressed. She said that practically any eleven-year-old bush kid could have done the same!

Kangawoos!
One of the young boys from a station near Meekatharra was taken to the Zoo in Perth by his parents. When he saw the kangaroos he turned to his dad and said with all the confidence that a three year old can muster, "Quick, Dad, get your gun—kangawoos." As the other visitors turned to stare disapprovingly, the boy's father edged away, in an attempt to temporarily disown his son. Interestingly, most kangaroo species are now more numerous than when white people arrived, because there are so many more watering points. Although some species are endangered, most people on the land are very conservation-minded nowadays, but kangaroos can reach plague proportions. At these times, a roo shooter is called in.

RFDS And SOTA
Before the time when the stations had the Digital Radio Compression System telephones (DRCS), every station would radio in to the Royal Flying Doctor Scheme (RFDS) each morning. At 6.45 am the base radio operator would go through the roll call. If people were going to be away they would tell the operator before leaving. This made the system a great safety net.

At set times during the day, any telegrams or messages would be given out by listing the call signs, so that people could then call in and receive their messages. In addition, telephone messages could be relayed both to and from stations throughout the day.

In the morning, the primary schooling service, the School of the Air (SOTA) would give each grade half an hour on the radio. The RFDS ran the radio equipment used by SOTA. The school sends out ten lessons to each student once a fortnight. The children would then work their way through the lessons under the supervision of their parents or their governess. The lessons were sent out on the fortnightly mail run and returned in the same way. The teacher would then correct and mark the lessons and return the marked work along with a new set of lessons. Each teacher had their class on air for just one half-hour lesson per day. In addition to the academic lessons, there might also be music lessons, Brownies of the air, or Parent and Citizen Meetings. In order to ensure the children had some social interaction with their peers each SOTA school would arrange extra activities such as camps, sports meetings, and other events. Meekatharra SOTA held activity days for various age groups, usually on one of the stations. They also held a week-long sports camp leading up to Sports Day in Meekatharra, where the SOTA students would participate alongside the Meekatharra District Primary and High School students.

SOTA also arranged a week-long seminar for mothers, governesses and students early in the year. Parents travel long distances and work very hard to get the children to the camps. However, if mustering or shearing is going on, it is virtually impossible to go to a camp. There is always someone shearing or mustering, so it is hard to make a date that suits everyone.

We often visited these events and took Gus along to entertain the kids.

Gus

Gus was the third member of our team. With a shock of bright red hair and a clown costume, Gus told the most terrible jokes, such as, 'Why did the chewing gum cross the road? It was stuck to the chicken's foot!' In spite of the awful jokes, he was greatly loved by all the children in the area. Gus was Bob's ventriloquist doll.

Bob & Gus

One day we forgot Gus and arrived at a station without him. Two children ran out to meet us, asking for Gus. When we explained that we had forgotten him, the children turned away and walked off greatly disappointed. We did not see them again all day! That's how important Gus was to the kids in our ministry. He was also important in the small congregations we had. Gus always found it very easy to keep the interest of kids in church!

Boarding School

A young station boy went off to boarding school at the age of 12. His parents had tried to teach him everything they thought he would need to know, including how to tie a school tie. But they had forgotten to teach him how to tie shoelaces! He had spent his childhood barefoot, or wearing elastic-sided boots or sandals, but he had never had lace-up shoes.

There are so many differences between being schooled through SOTA and going to boarding school. For a start, rather than having the freedom to create your own timetable, boarding school requires sitting for hours in a classroom, with set times to do particular work. In addition, you are surrounded by people all day every day, and all night every night, as the boarding houses require the students to sleep in dormitories. But perhaps the hardest thing for these young people is that they are very used to talking and relating to adults, while they have very limited interaction with people of their own age. They also have very limited experience playing team sports, with the once-a-year sports day being the main team time. However, bush children are resourceful and independent. As a result, they usually do very well when they go away for secondary school, even if it is hard on them and their parents. After being together for 24 hours a day 365 days a year, it is a very big wrench for the whole family to have to say goodbye when the academic year begins. A few families do carry on with correspondence at secondary level, rather than sending their children away to boarding school. The problems that can arise from this choice are the difficulties of coping with independent study, as well as the lack of social interaction with their peers.

1959

In 1984, the year before we went to the Murchison, Meekatharra SOTA celebrated twenty-five years in operation. One of the stories we heard was a memory of the first year of SOTA, in 1959. At the end of that year it had been decided that everyone would meet in Meekatharra, and the children would put on a concert. A great deal of practise went on over the radio. The great day dawned, with parents sitting waiting for the performance. The curtains opened to a stage set with the actors. At the sight of so many people, they froze. One mum had the presence of mind to rush onto the stage with an unplugged microphone in her hand, which she gave to the first speaker. As the children were so used to speaking into microphones, once he had the mic in his hand there was no further problem. He said his bit and then handed the mic on to the next speaker, and they continued in this vein until the concert was finished.

Help Me!

One day, the radio operator in Meekatharra heard a very young voice saying, 'Help me, help me, help me'. He asked who it was and where they where, and became increasingly worried when all he heard back was, 'help me' repeated over and over. This went on for about 15 minutes until suddenly another voice came on. The new voice sheepishly explained that she had left her young twins unattended for a few minutes while she was hanging out the washing. One of the twins had been using the radio to ask for help because her brother was hitting her! Even at two years old, she knew that if she was in trouble the RFDS radio was the place to go for help.

Guiding

When we first arrived in Meekatharra I happened to mention at church one day that I had been involved with the Girl Guides for some years. After church, a member of the congregation came bouncing up and announced that she was so pleased that I was about to start a Girl Guides group in Meekatharra. After an explanation that that was not possible as I would be away too often for that to happen, she announced that in that case she would run the group herself, if I helped her get started. I could hear my friends in SA laughing, as I had had told them that once we moved to Meekatharra there was no way I would be involved in Guiding, as I would be out with Bob too much!

As it turned out, we very quickly had both the Brownies and the Guides running in Meekatharra, and a short time later, both Brownies and Guides in Mount Magnet— a 200 kilometres drive from Meekatharra, along a narrow single-lane road. The road made for some interesting driving, with the road trains and the caravans that would use the road to drive north in the winter months. The locals would slow right down and drive off the sealed road whenever a road train or a caravan approached. This decision wasn't entirely selfless, as it meant there was less chance of a broken windscreen as you passed each other. Inexperienced drivers only put two wheels onto the dirt for these big vehicles, but very quickly learnt of the better method.

With all this Guiding going on, I became the District Commissioner for the Girl Guides. After about three years I handed over the reins, with two other Girl Guide leaders taking over as the District Commissioners of Meekatharra and Mount Magnet respectively. The same Brownie leader ran the Brownies group in Mount Magnet for the whole nine years that we were in the Murchison. Unfortunately, after a couple of years, the Girl Guide Leader from Mount Magnet moved away, and we could not find anyone to take her place. In Meekatharra, we had Brownies for most of the nine years we were there and Guides for about six years.

Guide camps were interesting. Camping on stations, out of sight of homesteads (but close enough in case of an emergency), made the girls feel as though they were really out in the middle of the bush. It was fun for all of us. At the first camp we ran, the girls were told about the importance of keeping their bed rolls well tied up and their tents tidy, in case any snakes and spiders decided to make their way into the camp. Although we didn't encounter either of those creatures, a large goanna—known locally as a bungarra—wandered into camp. He sauntered around between the tents, having a good look at all of the strange new additions to his landscape and sniffing everything in sight. I have never seen such a shipshape camp as the one we had after that! He must have spread the word, as a number of bungarras visited that camp in the following days, and over time the girls got over their fear and became very interested in them.

Girl Guides At End Of Camp

Brownie Adventures

In December 1986 we organised a Brownie Revels on a station. This is where a number of Brownie Units meet for a day and have a number of fun activities built around a theme. As Brownies from Meekatharra, Mount Magnet, Mullewa and Geraldton were all taking part, and since these units covered a distance of approximately 600 kilometres, we met at a station about 280 kilometres from Meekatharra. We all came dressed as swaggies, and the games were improvised around that theme. We threw nuts into billies hung from a tree branch, walked on jam tin stilts, sang Australian songs, threw horseshoes over a stick, along with many other similar activities.

On another occasion, Meekatharra Brownies went all the way to Perth for a Brownie Revels. They set off on the nine-hour bus trip after school on a Friday afternoon, ready for the revels the following day, before returning to Meekatharra on

Sunday, after a wonderful time. 115 kilometres from home, the bus broke down and they had to be towed home! Even though the leaders had rung with the news of the breakdown, a very worried District Leader was waiting for the girls in Meekatharra, but she was quickly able to set her worries to one side, as they all thought it a great adventure.

Air Activities
Not long before we left the Murchison I happened to say to Bob it was a pity it was so far to take the girls to Perth, as I would like to take them to an Air Activities day. I had taken some Guides to Geraldton for this event some years before, but since that time it had no longer been run there. Bob looked at me in surprise, and asked why I didn't simply run an Air Activities day myself, right there in Meekatharra.

Before anything else, we needed to get permission from headquarters, especially as we wanted to take the Brownies up for a flight as well as the Guides. The message came back that we could go ahead with the Air Activities day. And so the planning started in earnest. With thirty girls all wanting to have a flight, and only space for three at a time in the plane, we had to have other activities going.

The girls were placed in groups of six. Each group moved round, visiting each activity. Visits were arranged to the meteorological section and the RFDS. Other activities included making paper aeroplanes and seeing which one flew the best. There was also a mock search and rescue. We had a little toy plane, about three inches long, and they had to do a square search for it. The plane was red, so that it wouldn't be easily seen in the dirt. It came as a great surprise to the girls that it was so hard to find the toy. It opened their eyes to how difficult it could be to find a downed plane from the air—let alone a person.

The day dawned fine, but it was very windy and rough up in the plane. Even so, the girls loved it. All the girls had a plane ride and took part in each activity, and all the leaders who wanted to have a trip in the plane had a go.

Total Blindness

Bob's cousin came to visit with a friend who had total blindness. We all became so impressed with the way she managed everything. When she first arrived she walked round the house with her white cane, explaining that if we didn't move any furniture while she was staying with us, she wouldn't need to use her cane inside. She came flying with us and walked in the bush with us, impressing the station people with how well she coped. We had the Guides and Brownies meet with her, and they asked all sorts of questions and became very much more understanding of the problems faced by people with a disability.

CHAPTER 17

Animals: Jenny

Pigeons

We were visiting way out east of Wiluna one day, when a station manager caught an exhausted racing pigeon. We put the pigeon in a box and took him to Meekatharra, where we rang the Racing Pigeon Society in Perth. They traced the owner through the numbers on the metal band on the bird's legs. The owner was delighted, and was willing to pay the cost of sending the bird from Meeka to Perth. We were very interested to hear that the bird had been released at Iowna Station, south of Mount Magnet, and had been in a race to Perth. He was hundreds of kilometres off course. We happened to have been flying the day he was released, and measured winds of over 50 knots at 6,000 feet, even though the winds at ground level were quite light. Only the birds who habitually flew low made it to Perth.

Cattle

Some time later, on a visit to a different station, they were castrating and branding some of the cattle, and asked Bob if he would help. As there was only a young husband and wife tackling the job, the extra pair of hands was clearly going to make a great difference, so into the yard goes Bob. He was asked to help hold the young bull down, and shown where to hold it. He was then warned that when they had finished branding, he was to run for the fence as the steer would not be in an amenable mood. All went ahead, and Bob did his best to make a fast getaway. Even so, he was very nearly caught by the extremely angry steer. For the next ones, he moved even faster.

Wiluna Emu Farm
We had a very interesting Emu Farm at Wiluna. There are now many emu farms, but when we arrived in 1985 there was only one, staffed by one white man and several aboriginals. Initially, they had herded the emus together and thought they would pair off themselves. As female emus are solitary birds and the male makes the nest and rears the chicks, this did not work.

Besides, you cannot sex an emu by looking at it, only by feel after they are 12 months old. Something they do not appreciate.

The emu farmers had already discovered that they needed to put a male in a fenced-off area at breeding time, so that he could make his nest. After he had made his nest, they could then introduce a female. Once they had bred, she would lay about eight eggs. They would then give her to another male.

The females could lay up to 16 eggs, which was really too many for one male, and so they had a hatchery for extra eggs, and for any eggs that they found in the bush.

There was one male who was a bit old for nest sitting, so he would be given the job of looking after newly hatched chicks. He would walk around the farm very proudly with about 50 chicks in tow.

CHAPTER 18

Insects: Bob

Flies

In our patrol work, we came across giant centipedes, massed attacks by moths, and several different types of large ant. After rain, tiny biting insects known as "midgies" could raise quite disproportionate lumps under the skin that itched for weeks. Despite the name, March flies could be encountered at any time of the year, but only appeared in the rare good seasons. But the most pervasive insect in the outback is the small black fly. These pests gather near or on living creatures. They seek moisture in any crevices, such the eyes or nose. There was a saying amongst the Americans serving at Woomera that you could not claim to be an Aussie until you liked Vegemite and had swallowed your first fly. We already qualified on both counts before we went to Meekatharra, but our qualifications with the latter reached professorship level during our time there. Mostly though, these small bush flies are easily kept at bay by waving a hand or blowing a jet of air towards the afflicted area. Flies on the back, arms, or legs could be ignored.

Cockroaches

It is often said that the kids in Meekatharra use the cockroaches as skateboards. In fact, the wee beasties are only about five to six centimetres from nose to tail, and even the smallest kid would struggle to balance. Nevertheless, these cockroaches are about three times the length, width and depth of their city cousins. They are vegetarians, feeding on dead grasses and garden litter, and mostly keeping themselves to themselves. However, the situation when we first arrived in Meekatharra was not normal. The back lawn had not been watered for 12 months and there had been little or no rain. Not only was the lawn dead, but the ground had cracked open and allowed the cockroaches access to the septic tank below, where they had found ideal breeding conditions and multiplied alarmingly. As the lawn was dead, and therefore provided them with no food, they had penetrated to the inside of the house in search for food, which proved to be in vain, and so there they died. Despite constant cleaning, we would find two or three dead or near-dead cockroaches every morning for weeks. Baits merely acted as attractants. Fortunately it rained heavily not long after we arrived, and much to our surprise the lawn revived and the cracks in the ground closed up, cutting off the breeding chambers from the outside. The problem was greatly reduced, but we still had occasional cockroaches in the house for the whole nine years we lived there.

CHAPTER 19

Different Kinds Of Shooting: Bob

Firearms—A Blessing Or A Curse?
Even before the Port Arthur massacre in April 1996, a number of atrocities in America had caused many people both inside and outside the churches to call for stricter gun laws. Indeed, many Australians want a totally firearm-free society. How would this be viewed in the outback?

You will find pistols, rifles, and shotguns on every station. They are used for shooting injured stock or for shooting feral animals such as cats, dogs, donkeys, or camels. In days gone by they were used to shoot kangaroos for dog food—and no doubt a few still do this, despite the dangers of hydatids, not to mention the fact that it is no longer legal except for licenced 'roo shooters. But guns have a dark side. They can kill or maim people. In the bush, they are the preferred method for suicide or murder. And one small slip can lead to a tragic accident. One old-timer told me this story. Some of the details may have become blurred with the passing of time. Nevertheless, the essential facts are right.

In the 1930's, Mick, a young man with a vision of owning a cattle station, established a station south of the Pilbara. In those days you could still take up land for pastoral purposes, although all the best land had been grabbed many years before. He took work anywhere he could get it, so as to gather enough money to build a homestead and buy some cattle. He was able to move permanently onto the station after the war, but money was always a problem. To supplement his meagre income from the station, he took on a contract to care for part of the rabbit-proof fence that passed thorough the station. One day, in the early 50's, he was riding along the fence when he noticed a hole near ground level. To repair it he would have to get through to the other side. So he got off his horse and gathered his tools and his gun and crawled under the fence. Unfortunately, as he pulled his paraphernalia through behind him, the trigger of the gun caught on something and the gun went of, shooting him in the abdomen. There he was, miles from home and badly injured. Mick was made of pretty stern stuff. He crawled back through the fence, somehow got on his horse, and let the horse take him home.

On arrival, he struggled inside and got on the pedal radio to Meekatharra, where the Royal Flying Doctor Service had recently established a base. Unfortunately, their only plane, a modified Tiger Moth, was away. They said they would ask the patrol padre if he would go. Reverend Don McCaskill had a Tiger Moth which he had had modified to take a stretcher so he could stand in for the Flying Doctor in an emergency. So Don flew to the station, landed in a small clearing, and somehow got Mick onto the stretcher in the plane. He landed right outside the hospital at Meekatharra and, nine hours after the accident, Mick was given medical care.

Some weeks later he was transferred to Perth where he made a slow recovery. I met Mick in about 1987 when he was nearly 80 years of age. He was a great supporter of Frontier Services and a great advocate of gun safety. He died of a heart attack at the age of 84.

One murder, one attempted murder, and two suicides

involving guns happened during our time in the patrol ministry. But I must say that the vast majority of station people are very careful and responsible with their firearms. They know the dangers and support tough gun laws. However, they would never be able to contemplate a life without their firearms. They are neither a blessing nor a curse. They are just like many other tools of their trade – dangerous if mishandled but a necessity for the work they do.

CHAPTER 20

Photography: Jenny

One afternoon, not long after we arrived in Meekatharra, the phone rang. It was an American named Michael O'Brian, calling from New York. He was a famous portrait photographer and wanted to come to Meekatharra to take photos for an upcoming book, entitled *A Day In The Life Of Australia*, which was to include photographs of Australians taken by 100 of the world's leading photographers. He had previously been to Meekatharra when our predecessor was there, doing a job for National Geographic about the bicentennial. His belief was that if you wanted to see real Australians, Meekatharra was the place to go.

We duly arranged for him and his assistant to come and stay with us for a week, which would give him time to photograph enough people to provide a wide selection to choose from for his contribution to the book.

During the time Michael was with us, we would leave the house at about eight o' clock in the morning, straight after breakfast, and fly him out to several stations, arriving back as it was getting dark, for dinner and a good night's sleep, before starting all over again the next day. As well as flying out to all the stations, he spent one day in Meekatharra, and was very excited to find three Aboriginal girls that he had photographed on his last visit. He photographed them again. This picture was one of the three of Michael's photos chosen for the book.

Michael was most impressed that I prepared home-cooked meals each day, and towards the end of the week he asked if he could take us out to dinner in Meekatharra. We told him that we thought the Imperial Hotel had the best cook at that time.

After a roast dinner and sweets at the Imperial, Michael turned to Bob and quietly asked about tipping. Bob's reply was, 'Oh we don't tip in Australia unless the service is outstanding.'

The service was fine, but I would not have called it outstanding. Old habits die hard, though, and Michael left a couple of two-dollar notes under his plate. As we were walking out, the waiter came running after us, exclaiming, "Excuse me, mate, you left these on the table. "

Michael blushed deeply and stammered, "That's the tip."

The waiter scratched his head for a moment, before saying, "Gee, thanks mate..."

Afterwards, Michael remarked that you could be embarrassed for *not* tipping in the US, but he didn't know you could be embarrassed *for* tipping in Australia.

CHAPTER 21

The Races: Jenny

Each town in our patrol had one horserace day each year, followed the next day by a gymkhana for their horses. Even very young children took part in this. We always attended these races with enjoyment.

However, each year in the Murchison, a very important race carnival took place. This consisted of two afternoons of races and two mornings of polocrosse and a gymkhana in between those events. Bob went to every Landor race in our time there, but I missed one when I was in the Solomon Islands.

This traditional event began in 1921 at a mustering camp with a number of stockmen from stations in the area. As the legend goes, the stockmen were resting on their day off, when they started to argue who had the fastest horse. Arising from this vibrant discussion, stockmen from the surrounding stations formed the EGRC and the Landor Races were born.

Since then, the event has run annually except for several years during the Second World War, and is strictly an amateur meeting. There are no starting gates, all races being a walk up start. The race meeting is open to RWWA registered horses, that is horses bred above the 28th parallel, corn fed, and have not won a race on a metropolitan track. Mostly all the horses are ridden by station employees. Others must be approved by the committee and must be an amateur rider.

When we arrived in the Murchison, we were invited to camp with one of our stations, and from then on everyone knew that was where we would be camping. On the Thursday before the races, we arrived in our Urvan, and parked around the campsite. There were many tents and caravans, and some just threw their gear on the ground to sleep in. At mealtimes, we congregated in the roof-covered area that also had a table and refrigerator. More importantly, it had two sides of corrugated iron to shelter from the prevailing wind. But mostly we seated around a campfire to the east of the main area.

Thursday evening was a free sausage sizzle for early comers eager to catch up on news and gossip. Then over the course of the next few days, events were held in the biggest of the three halls. On Friday evening it was the children's party, followed by two-up and drinking after the children had gone to bed, readying everyone for the main race on Saturday afternoon.

On Saturday morning, polocrosse was played, followed by the afternoon races, with the Ladies Bracelet the main race. Then, after the races were completed, the Ball began, with some people dancing all night.

Landor Races

On Sunday morning till lunchtime was the gymkhana for under 14 girls and boys who were 10 and under. At midday it was the declaration of Acceptors for the Landor Cup, followed by ladies and gentlemen riding in the gymkhana, a tug of war, and desert dash. Later in the evening, it was the presentation for the gymkhana trophy and Calcutta for the Landor Cup.

The event continued into Monday, with morning polocrosse and afternoon races, the main race being the Landor Cup. Then after the EGRC trophy presentation, the bar was opened for anyone interested in dancing the night away again.

Landor Gymkhana

Adjacent to the big hall where all the main events were held was the smallest grandstand I have seen. South of the bar was a similar hall where the CWA provided tea and coffee, and where pies and meals were sold. Somewhere in all this mix, Bob was expected to put on a church service. We tried various times, which often meant different people could attend in between looking after their horses and cooking at their camp site. It was a hectic time, but also a wonderful for people who often only saw each other once a year. Bob and I always had a great time catching up with everyone.

On one occasion at the races, while we were sitting round the campfire having a pre-dinner drink, small children were playing around beside me saying something that neither myself nor my neighbour were listening to. I felt something on my feet, as I only had sandals on, and as I looked down and started to lift the back of my foot up, I realised a dugite snake had just rolled off my feet. My neighbour had the fastest reaction possible and had the snake held down just behind its head with his riding boot. Another man rushed over with a spade and very quickly dispatched it. The dugite snake is a venomous and potentially lethal snake native to WA. We then realised what the small children had been saying, "Nake! Nake!"

As we always had a RFDS plane on stand bye for the week end anyone if bitten would have been quickly helped.

CHAPTER 22
Holidays: Jenny

Most years while we were at Meekatharra, we spent our holidays exploring Western Australia. In 1989 we drove the Urvan up to the Kimberley. On the Gibb River Road we called in at a station for fuel. The mechanic at the service station invited us to stay the night, as they had not had a patrol padre for some time.

Being on holiday, we said we wanted to press on. As we were leaving, we got a flat tyre. The mechanic seemed happier about this turn of events than we were, but we ended up having a very enjoyable night with lots of chatter, and some good advice.

As I had been bitten by midges just before we left in Meekatharra, I had large welts on my legs. I was informed that mixing equal parts Dettol and baby oil would stop anything except the small bush fries from attacking me. I have sworn by the formula ever since.

Extract From A Letter Written in 1989 by Bob

I don't often complain about the hardships of the job, but I make an exception this once. At Easter time, Jenny and I had to go to Cocos Island to minister to the Christian group there for two whole weeks! They even made me play golf and made both of us go snorkelling. AND they only provided us with one motorcar for our use.

On the plus side, they let me conduct seven services—six, anyway, as the sunrise Service on Easter Day was washed out by the only thunderstorm of our visit.

Seriously, the trip a great time and very worthwhile. The strong Christian group there only have visiting ministers four times a year, with a different denomination on each occasion, and so they make good use of the time. For our part, we found inspiration in their faithfulness in such an isolated outpost of Australia. We made many friends.

Cocos (Keeling Island)

We arrived on Cocos Island and walked over to the car that we had been loaned for the duration of our stay. We went to put our case in the boot.

"Stop," the locals pleaded. "If you put your case in there it may fall through—the boot is so rusty!"

We put the case on the back seat.

As I approached the passenger side of the car they said, "Wait a moment, Jenny, don't step in before you sit down, or you may go through the floor. The foot well is so rusty!"

The car was only four years' old, and had only been on the island for two years. But as the island was only about ten feet above sea level, the salt air plays havoc with anything that is made of metal!

I wonder how the island is faring in the changing climate.

Another interesting fact about the island that we quickly discovered is that if you are playing golf and a siren goes off, you must stop playing and leave the course—as it crosses the landing strip for the planes.

No one on the island plays golf when the fortnightly plane is due to come in.

Cocos (Keeling Island)

CHAPTER 23
Baptisms & Weddings: Jenny

Weddings

Bob's first two weddings took place within our first few months in the patrol, both in the April of that year. The first was on a station out past Wiluna, on the edge of the desert. It was a very traditional wedding with all the trimmings, and was a great way to mark their marriage as their life together may never include another event of such formality. There were 200 guests, many of whom had either flown or driven very long distances. With so many people, it was decided that the service would have to be held outside. Fortunately, the weather was kind and everything went off very well.

The second wedding was the more eventful of the two. As the station did not have landing strip we made the drive over, rather than flying in. We pulled up at the homestead, where we were greeted by a young man, who informed us that we were to go down to the mine. We made our way down to the mine, where we were met by a very bright and vivacious young woman.

"You're the minister?" she said to Bob.

"I am indeed," he confirmed.

"You'll do," she announced, after looking him up and down.

It turned out that the couple in question wanted to get married on the mine, but as both were divorced, neither the Catholic priest nor the Anglican priest would conduct the service, and the registrar at Cue would only perform the ceremony in the nearby town.

After some discussion it was agreed that Bob would conduct the wedding. When he asked what date they had in mind, they said one month and one day from that date, which was the latest that the forms could be signed without getting a special licence.

Dump Truck Similar to Wedding Truck

The day dawned, with a pig cooking on a spit. The bride arrived in a huge dump truck, and emerged wearing a lovely dress and high heels. The cabin was almost four metres above the ground, but she climbed down with great poise and daintiness. The wedding went off very well, although the groom had broken his promise to wear his teeth for the occasion, as they were too painful. It was the biggest social event the place had ever known, with the mine decorated with bunting, streamers, and paper flowers. Even the dump truck was decorated.

As a result of that wedding we ended up with a church

service at the mine once a month for over a year, until the people attending it all moved away.

Baptisms

The problems that outback people have with the churches over baptisms for their children are unbelievable. One minister asked a couple to attend church for 12 weeks in a row before he would even consider baptising their child. The round trip to church was 450 kilometres, and, as a result, the child had not been baptised when we arrived at the station. This was not unusual. Bob said he wondered what Jesus would have said.

Not long after we arrived in Meekatharra, Bob was on the telephone, arranging our second visit to one of the stations, when he heard a voice in the background saying, "Tell him to bring his branding iron." It was the station owner's father, and he was referring to a baptism, which Bob duly agreed to perform, while I was to take the role of videographer.

When we arrived everything was set up on the verandah, with a tablecloth over the meat chopping block to serve as the pedestal for the baptismal font, and a bowl on top to hold the water.

There were two brothers taking part in the service – the older boy was aged about three, and his younger brother was about eighteen months. We all gathered, and Bob made the mistake baptising the baby first. The problem wasn't with the baby, however. The baptism went smoothly enough, but the three year old had been watching the proceedings carefully, and decided it was not for him. When Bob turned to the boy, the child took off at a fast clip with his grandfather in hot pursuit, while I continued to film it all for posterity. The boy took a bit of catching, but eventually the deed was done.

Afterwards, over a cuppa, the grandfather told us a story of being in the Kimberley, many years before. A stranger sat watching as the grandfather branded cattle. After a while, the grandfather said to the stranger "What do you do for a crust?" The bloke replied, "I'm in much the same game as you. I muster as many as I can and put my brand on them. I'm a Catholic priest."

Baptisms were always great occasions, and though it was only the family present when the two young boys were baptised, most of the baptisms created the opportunity to throw a party with many friends flying and driving in. In one three-month period in 1990 we had seven baptisms, some of which even had people flying in from overseas to witness the reception of a child into the family of God.

An important feature of station baptisms is the ecumenical dimension. The UCA, the Catholics, the Anglicans, and the Lutherans all agreed to recognise baptisms carried out by one another.

During the road patrol from Exmouth we had a very special baptism on the beach at sunrise. Before this, our first baptism in the Exmouth Patrol was a triple baptism for three siblings. The children's baptism had been delayed for some time, as the eldest child had Asperger's syndrome and had not built a relationship with previous ministers. However, on our first visit to the station he enjoyed Bob's company, and later announced to his family that he wanted Bob to baptise him.

The day duly arrived, and, as usual, we took a picture Bible as a gift for the family, to mark the occasion. On this occasion, Bob made sure to baptise the eldest child first, before his sister and brother. The baptism took place by a lovely pool under a gum tree. As soon as the first baptism was completed, Bob gave the boy the picture Bible. He immediately sat in the red dirt, completely absorbed in reading it.

Another very special baptism was also a triple. This family only had one girl, aged seven. However, some years before, Bob was to have baptised her two male cousins on a station north of Meekatharra. In the end, it never happened because they moved further north, out of our patrol area, and we lost touch with them. Once they heard that the children's cousin was to be baptised, they travelled over so that their boys could also take part. Both mothers had prepared their children vey well. To mark the occasion, the little girl had made a picture of what she thought the baptism would be like. It was a remarkable drawing. The water and the garden scene were beautifully portrayed. After a special meal and party for all visitors we stayed the night. The next morning at breakfast one of the boys said to his younger cousin, " I can't see the cross on your forehead."

"No. But I know it's there," she quietly replied.

CHAPTER 24

Funerals: Bob

John Ford was the most conservative man I ever met. All his life he stubbornly resisted change of any sort. His sheep station was reached by a long track off the main road. Twenty years after kilometres replaced miles as our measure of distance, a faded hand-painted sign proclaimed: "Paroo – 20 miles." It was still there when he died.

I used to drop in at Paroo about twice a year. The airstrip was not very good, but the track from the main road was punctuated by five old-fashioned gates and was usually very rough. Besides, the trip by air was only thirty minutes from Meekatharra and the road trip took at least an hour and a half.

John was a very devout Anglican, but he always made Jenny and me feel very welcome. He would usually ask me to conduct a service in the little mudbrick chapel he had built next to the homestead. The only condition was that I would use the 1662 Church of England Book of Common Prayer. This I was always pleased to do, and the whole family and staff would attend.

About seven years after I first met him, John called at the manse in Meekatharra and calmly told me that he was suffering from terminal cancer, and had only about a year to live. He wanted to discuss his ideas for his funeral. He wanted four clergy to officiate: an Anglican bishop from Perth, two Anglican priests who had occasionally called at Paroo over the years, and me. I was quite flattered to be asked, especially in view of the fact that John had always been such a staunch Anglican. Of course, I readily agreed.

John made very careful preparations for his death. He rewrote his will. He had a booklet printed with the whole funeral service in it. Basically, it was a combination of the services for the Burial of the Dead and the extended version of Holy Communion and several other bits and pieces from the 1662 Book of Common Prayer. There were four hymns, and it would obviously take at least an hour. He went through all the legal procedures that were needed so that his burial could be on the station. A beautiful shady site was chosen on the banks of the West Creek, about a mile north of the homestead. In recognition of his many years of service as a councillor, the shire council agreed to grade the road into Paroo and to send a front-end loader to dig the grave when the time came. One of his daughters took a year off from her nursing job in England to care for him in his last months.

Finally, many months later, after he was satisfied that all possible arrangements had been made, and nothing could go wrong, John died peacefully in Meekatharra District Hospital. The funeral arrangements were set in train the next day.

The first problem was in deciding a date which would suit everyone. There were John's eight children, most of whom had left home and had family responsibilities. There were the four clergy, the police (who would act as undertakers), the shire, and all the neighbours for hundreds of kilometres around. It was difficult, but finally a suitable day was found on a Monday, nine days after John died.

The next little problem was that the shire authorities

declared that their ancient hearse would not be capable of making the long journey to Paroo and back. The family was very disappointed, until one councillor had the bright idea that the hearse could be transported on a six-wheel car-trailer which he owned. The council agreed. Bush people are good at overcoming problems. John's plans were back on track. But worse was to come. Robert Burns wrote that the best laid plans of mice and men oft do go aglae, and things began to go aglae in a big way on the night before the funeral.

It rained heavily during the night, and first thing in the morning an anxious family found that the grave, so carefully dug by the council a few days earlier, was now under water. The West Creek had overflowed. The track from the homestead to the gravesite was impassable. The funeral would have to be postponed. Doris, John's wife of forty years went to the telephone to begin the long task of letting everyone know that the funeral was off. The phone was dead. Water had entered the steel box full of wonderful new technology, and it was kaput. The short wave radio, which had long been their only contact with civilisation, had failed about a year earlier. It had never been repaired because the telephone was so much better—at least it had been until it died. John Ford would have laughed. He never trusted these newfangled things anyway.

The first person to arrive for the funeral came at ten o'clock. He didn't know what time the funeral was (1 o'clock) and came early so as to be sure not to miss it. His four-wheel-drive was equipped with a new short-wave radio. At the family's request, he contacted the Royal Flying Doctor Service at Meekatharra and asked them to urgently advise as many people as possible that the funeral was off. I got a call from the operator about

10.30 am asking me to tell the other clergy. I rang the bishop in Perth and caught him just before he left home to take a chartered flight from Jandakot. One of the others was already in Meekatharra and was to fly out with me, but the fourth one was already on his way and didn't answer my calls.

Meanwhile, many more people were on their way. Jenny was not able to come as she was in hospital. By midday, when the family was sitting at lunch on a hill near the homestead, a steady stream of guests began to pull in. The hearse arrived, on the low loader, towed by a council truck. Doris called a hasty family conference. They decided that the service in the chapel should go ahead and that the actual burial could be a small family affair when the gravesite dried out. Once again, the short wave radio was enlisted and RFDS was asked to crank up the arrangements again for a service at 2 o'clock.

I immediately rang the bishop. He was unimpressed, but agreed to try to charter a fast plane and get there as soon as he could. I rang my Anglican colleague and said, "Guess what? It's on again!"

"Can I still come with you?" he asked.

"Sure" I said, "but you will need to be here at the house by ten to one."

He agreed.

The flight to Paroo was uneventful. There were just a few isolated showers around, and we were soon in the circuit over Paroo. It was obvious that the downpour which had caused so many problems was fairly localised. Dust was still rising from parts of the road, but the area near the homestead was slick with the legacy of the storm. Water does not soak quickly into that hard red ground and pools glistened in all the slight depressions. The overflow from the West Creek had spread about halfway towards the homestead. There were a few pools on the airstrip, but I knew the ground underneath would be rock-hard because the strip was just a straight part of the road and years of traffic had compacted the already hard ground. I waited for a gap in the stream of cars and landed towards the house.

There were about 60 vehicles parked higgledy-piggledy under the shade of the trees near the chapel. Mud spattered the sides and clung damply to the undersides. The crowd of mourners, mostly men, stood in groups making nervous conversation. The chapel seemed to have an invisible fence around it. Nobody wanted to be the first to go in. Inside, all was ready. The old pews had been dusted. Flowers graced the tiny sanctuary area. The coffin, draped with an Australian flag, was balanced on a long stool just in front of the altar rail. It seemed almost a shame to intrude modern technology into the simple solemnity of the scene. I set up a microphone and ran a lead to the portable amplifier outside. The Catholic nun was to set up and play the portable organ near the back of the chapel, and we ran another lead from it out to the amplifier. Then we all stood outside watching the sky and waiting for the bishop to arrive.

After a while, it was obvious that the weather was deteriorating and the bishop wasn't going to make it. I asked Doris what we should do. "

"If he is not here by three o'clock, I suppose we'd better start", she said.

The other two parsons and I hurriedly divided the service

up between us and went to change into ecclesiastical dress. With a little bit of chivvying, we persuaded people to go into the chapel. Fifty people crammed in, and more than 100 people stood outside near the amplifier. Promptly, at three o'clock, we started the service.

Nearly an hour later, as I was reading the last of the Scripture passages (the whole of Second Corinthians Chapter 15), there was a deafening clap of thunder. People started to look around nervously. I speeded up the reading. As soon as the service ended, people began to leave in a hurry. I collected the electronic gear as quickly as I could and ran for the aeroplane. Outside the chapel, the cause of the thunder was immediately obvious. A great storm was only about two kilometres off, and coming our way. Torrential rain was sheeting from the bottom of the roiling cloud. I threw the gear into the back of the aeroplane and my colleague and I clambered into the cabin. The aeroplane started first time and I taxied to the take-off point. Cars were already moving down the strip. I did a very quick warm-up and check, and as soon as a gap came in the traffic we took off. We had to fly a long way to get round the storms but we made it safely back to Meekatharra and landed just before the mother of all thunderstorms hit the town. We were still tying down the aeroplane when it reached the aerodrome. We got very wet, but were glad to be home safely.

Meanwhile, the people who had driven into Paroo were having all sorts of troubles as they tried to leave. The hearse, which had never been unloaded from the low loader, was amongst the first to get away. The cars behind it could not pass and formed a long convoy in the blinding rain. Disaster struck about fifteen miles from the station where the West Creek crosses the track. It was quite deep by the time the truck and hearse got there. The truck went slowly into the water. Right in the middle of the creek, it broke through the hard crust and sank to the chassis in mud. The engine stalled. It was to be there for over four months. The four-wheel drive vehicles all managed to get round the obstruction by leaving the road and ploughing separate tracks across the flood. They all got home, despite nearly eighty kilometres of flooded road, and the trip taking about five hours instead of the usual one and a half. At about eight o' clock that evening one exhausted friend in a four-wheel drive called in, needing a bed for the night. The conventional vehicles all turned back for the station.

I rang Doris the next day. She told me that there were thirty people stranded at Paroo. The strip was too wet to land on, but she thought that it might be possible the next day. I asked if she needed any food to feed the multitude, but she said all she needed was bread. I said I would bring some with me and fly out any of the people who wanted to go. She said that the bishop was very anxious to get out. "

"The bishop!" I exclaimed. "When did he get there?"

"He arrived just as the storm hit!" she replied.

Apparently his pilot had not liked the look of the strip for his big fast aeroplane, and had dropped the bishop at Wiluna. It had taken him an hour to get a lift from a mate and then a further hour to drive the 80 kilometres to the station.

After speaking to Doris, anxious about the coffin and its contents, I rang the police.

"Ah, no worries, padre," the sergeant said. "It was never in the hearse. We took it out and brought it back in the four-wheel drive. Old John is safely back in the morgue up at the hospital."

I rang Doris every few days to see when we might have the second part of the funeral – the burial. The story was always the same. The grave was still under water and the track impassable. Then, one day, about seven weeks later, I got a call from the hospital administrator.

"We've got a problem," he said, "and I hope you will be able to fix it."

He stammered and stuttered a bit, but the gist of what he told me was that the refrigeration at the morgue was not quite up to scratch and John's remains were starting to deteriorate.

"Well, what do want me to do about it?" I said.

"Um, well, we thought you might ring up the family and, er, suggest you could bury him temporarily at Meekatharra cemetery and then dig him up and rebury him on the station later on."

"I'll see what I can do," I said gloomily.

I rang an acquaintance in Perth who was in the undertaking business and asked him what he thought of the idea.

"Don't even think about it," he said. "Coffins these days are all made out of chipboard. After a couple of days in the ground they are too weak to support the body. Why don't you send him down to Perth and we'll cremate him?"

I rang Doris and told her all of this. She would not hear of a cremation. "John was dead against them," she said with unconscious irony. "And anyway, the family have been talking and we have more or less decided that it has all gone on too long. We think we ought to have him buried at Meekatharra and be done with it."

A wave of relief washed over me. It would be so simple, I thought. "Well, all right," I said, "if you are quite sure."

We talked about suitable days and she said that she would let me know as soon as she could.

Later that day, Doris rang me and told me the only day that would suit everyone was the following Monday. She sounded tired and I asked her how she was coping. "I'm all right," she said, "but I'll really be glad when it's all over."

"Surely nothing will go wrong now," I said.

"No. Let's hope not anyway," Doris replied.

But there were still a few more things to go aglae.

I was up a ladder at the church fixing a window, which had been broken in a terrible hailstorm a few weeks earlier, when Jenny came running from the manse to say that Doris was on the phone in a terrible state.

"Apparently the police will all be away on Monday and they can't do the funeral. But I said you'd fix it."

I don't usually use even minor profanities, but I was stunned.

"Fix it! How the heck am I going to fix it?" I said.

What was I going to say? Then I had an inspiration. I knew a man, now living in Meekatharra, who had once acted as undertaker for his father's funeral at Sandstone. When I suggested to Doris that I try to get him to do the job, she was very pleased. I rang this chap and explained the problem to him and asked if he would act as undertaker. "

"No trouble, Father Bob," (he was a Catholic and always called me that), "but what are we going to use for a hearse?"

I had forgotten that the hearse was still bogged fast in the West Creek.

"Leave that to me." I said. "If you will do the undertaking, I'll find a big dark-coloured station wagon that we can use."

We left it at that and I rang Doris with the good news. She was quite effusive with her thanks.

After many phone calls, I gave in on big, dark station wagons. The only thing available for the job would my own white Magna station wagon, and I hoped it would be big enough. After going up to the hospital and getting the key for the morgue, I did some careful measurements. I thought it might just fit. Surely no more could go wrong?

The burial was almost an anticlimax. Things went quite well. The coffin was too long to go in the vehicle except on the diagonal, but we had enough flowers to hide it completely and I doubt if anyone noticed. Our amateur undertaker positioned the coffin with the head at the eastern end of the grave, but the pallbearers soon turned it around, and the service went without a hitch. The bishop was there and there was a very large crowd.

The scene after the funeral was amazing. I have never been to another funeral where people stood around telling yarns and laughing after the service. I suppose everyone had done their grieving in the eight weeks between the chapel service and the final lowering of the casket into the grave. The relief was palpable. John was finally buried. Just about everyone had a tale to tell about him, and the heroic efforts it had taken to bury him! Doris had the last word.

"That was typical John Ford. He always said if was easy, it couldn't be any good!"

Eight years later, I was amazed to get a cutting from the West Australian newspaper saying that John Ford's body had been exhumed and finally put to rest just where he had wanted it to be.

"John always got his way," said Doris.

Four Funerals And A Wedding

Over a period of eleven days in July 1989 we had four funerals and a wedding, as well as a visit from the president elect of the UCA, a presbytery meeting, an induction of a new minister, and two Sunday services.

It began with the funeral of a very well-known and highly respected aboriginal. Our very good friend, the Reverend Don McCaskill, came up for the service, and Bob and Don shared the service. The next day, the two men flew down to Perth, as the aeroplane needed urgent attention to the brakes. They had lunch together, and then Bob flew home, landing soon after dark.

On arrival back at Meeka, he received a message saying Don had died that afternoon. The next day, we flew to a station for a wedding with 150 people in attendance. The following day, Bob conducted the service at the funeral of a well-known elderly lady. The day after that, we flew to Perth for Don's funeral. It was a beautiful occasion, and Bob also took part in the service for Don. We returned home the next day, as we had another funeral the day after in Meeka. This time it was for a very dear ninety-five year old lady.

After the funeral, we changed and went to the airport to pick up the president elect of the UCA—the Reverend D'arcy

Wood, who had been a lecturer when Bob was in Parkin Wesley College.

The next day, we flew to Karratha for a presbytery meeting, which included an induction service that Bob conducted. He was still putting the finishing touches to his sermon at midnight the night before!

In the midst of this we had friends staying with us, and we somehow managed to show them around a bit. They attended a School of the Air Activities Day, and I took them to the emu farm at Wiluna. Maxine also played the organ at church, which everyone enjoyed. I was particularly happy about that.

1989 we hired a Cessna 210—big brother to our Cessna 182—for a journey to take our boss, the Reverend Gray Birch, and three senior members of the Federal Council of the Royal Flying Doctor Service, to visit all the Flying Doctor bases and Frontier Service outposts in the state.

We visited Kalgoorlie, Wiluna, Meeka, Tom Price, Karratha, Port Hedland, Broome, Derby, Fitzroy Crossing, Halls Creek, Kununurra, Wyndham, Exmouth, and Carnarvon. We slept in a different bed almost every night, and met so many people it was hard to sort them out. It was a great flying experience in a very capable aeroplane, although we did run into an unexpected hitch before we even left the ground.

At that time, the usual allowance of weight for a passenger was seventy-seven kilos. The expectation is that some people will be under and some over, but it usually balances out. Bob and I were both well under the seventy-seven kilo limit, but three of our passengers weighed ninety kilos and the fourth was one-hundred-and-ten kilos.

This made for some interesting maths to work out how much fuel to take on for each leg. Luckily, for our longest leg, flying from Kununurra to Broome, one of our passengers was flying back to Perth from Kununurra, which both lowered the overall weight and enabled us to take on more fuel.

CHAPTER 25

The Plane: Jenny

Reading And Writing

When we first joined the patrol there were very few televisions, as nobody had twenty-four hour power. As a result, books were most important. We sent a message through our newsletter that we would love some books, so that we could take them around with us to the stations. Very quickly, we had ten box loads of books, and had to call a halt on more for a while. However, our mobile library proved to be very popular! There was one station in particular where the books were well received, as both the mother and daughter loved to read. The only drawback was that they also loved to write, and had 300 penfriends between them. This meant that we didn't always have a great deal of room to take many books if we were also delivering their mail! As the station was very isolated, they were not on a regular fortnightly mail run. This meant we sometimes filled the back of the plane with mail, after telling the post office we were going to be calling in two days before, so that they could get the bags of mail ready.

Services

In our early days with the patrol, Bob was conducting two services at Meekatharra every week, a service at Cue every fortnight, and one a month at both Mount Magnet and Wiluna. Gradually this changed, with the Anglicans conducting a Mount Magnet service every week, with fortnightly services at Cue and monthly services at Meekatharra. After this, we changed to every week at Meeka and once a month at Mount Magnet, Wiluna, Sandstone, and Yalgoo. This meant two services every Sunday! We had suggested to the Anglican ministers that we close our church when they were visiting our town, and vice versa, but unfortunately that never happened.

Sandstone was the most eventful of our Sunday services. We would fly down once a month, and Bob would conduct the service at the little Anglican church, half of which had fallen down. The only other church in town was the Catholic church, which we had been told was in very bad nick, that the doors had long since fallen off and that since then the only congregation had been the local goats and sheep.

However, one Sunday a baptism needed to be conducted in the Catholic church, and so the fire brigade hosed out the animal droppings and the shire clerk paid to have new doors fitted, which was reasonable as it was his children who were being baptised. These simple improvements revealed that the building was, in fact, in remarkably good condition. After that, Father Bertus offered us the use of the church whenever we wanted.

Our congregation was a bit reluctant to use the Catholic church, but when the roof hadn't fallen on us by the end of the first service they warmed up to the change of venue, and were even more enthusiastic when the other half of the Anglican church fell down a few weeks later.

Our first dawn Anzac service was held just outside Meekatharra, at a place called Peace Valley. It was well attended, and the setting in amongst great diorite rocks helped with the solemnity of the occasion. However, it proved so popular that so many people wanted to come to future services it needed to be moved to a different location, and from then on were held in front of the shire offices.

As well as the patrol, the UCA Church is organised into local areas called Presbyteries, which holds about three meetings a year, state meetings called synods, which hold annual meetings, and national meetings called assemblies, which take place every three years. As we had an aeroplane, we would often fly to one of the other towns and pick up a couple of people to attend the presbyteries. Included in the presbytery of the north west was Port Hedland, Karratha, Exmouth, Carnarvon, and Tom Price—as well as Meekatharra. It is the largest presbytery in Australia in area, but with the smallest number of ministers, with just five ministers covering about an eighth of the total land mass of Australia. At the time when we were with the patrol, our patrol—the Murchison Patrol—covered about half of that area. This patrol has since grown larger, and is covered by a four-wheel drive, rather than aeroplane.

We did not use the plane for everything, and in the early years with the patrol we used our Urvan on many occasions as an alternative to flying in to the stations, as it proved a very suitable vehicle for the roads, with a high clearance and comfortable sleeping platform. We had bought a foot-operated shower, and used to use it next to the fire when we were camping, as there are no tall trees in that area on which to hang a shower bucket. One evening a snake came to share my shower, until I told it rather crossly that snakes don't came out at night! In fact, it was my mistake, rather than the snake's, as this one was mulga snake—and they do come out a night.

Camping in Urvan

With or without the addition of the local wildlife, the nights spent camping in the van, as well as those spent sleeping under the wing of the plane, were unforgettable, under the majesty of the Australian night sky, which was filled with endless stars.

Old Man Kangaroo
Bob would always say that he had the best job in Australia. He would say that he divided his time between visiting some of the nicest people in the land, drinking tea, talking, and flying. I must say, I agreed with him—especially once I also learnt to fly.

However, the first year we were with the patrol, we were making one last visit on Christmas Eve when, just as we were about to touch down for landing, a large kangaroo bounded out of a bush and ran right into us. He missed the right wheel and the nose wheel, but hit the left wheel and left undercarriage, causing quite a bit of damage. What a fright we got! As Bob was a skilled pilot he straightened the plane and landed safely.

There had been such a loud bang that they had heard it at the homestead, over one kilometre away.

When we did not taxi up to the homestead the owner came down and found us surveying the damage. He and Bob then went off to ring our engineer in Perth, who informed Bob that if the damage had knocked the alignment out by even one centimetre that we were not to fly the plane. After returning with a tape measure, they measured from nose wheel to right wheel, then nose wheel to left wheel. However, it is very hard to measure in the field. Finally, Bob made the decision that it would be okay.

Once we had returned to Meeka, we had to think about getting the plane to Perth. It is very expensive to send a plane by road, so we decided to fly it down between Christmas and New Year—although we had noticed eleven rivets were missing.

We left at first light, when it was very calm.

When we got to Perth, our engineer informed us that the alignment was out by half an inch – about one and a quarter centimetres.

We were lucky to have made it to Perth. Unfortunately, what was not so lucky was that the cost of the repairs was going to be $3,500, and would take about eight weeks, as the spare parts needed to be sent from America. As for the very big old man kangaroo, he was killed instantly.

Heavy Rain

After heavy rain flying can get very interesting, as station strips often become soft, and are frequently damaged, and a number of strips have their width and length severely reduced. A careful look at a strip was required to ensure we were able to land and take off safely. One strip we landed on, the grader had been bogged eight times as the manager tried to repair the damage from the rain and floods. This meant that we were left with a length of 350 metres and a width of just 9 metres to land on, but we managed to make do with this pocket-handkerchief and landed safely. However, there were two occasions when we became bogged after heavy rain, with one wheel becoming completely stuck. In both cases it was all hands to help get us back on to firmer ground. But we were able to return the favour, as for a few weeks after heavy rains many strips were covered in long grass and flowers. This meant our propeller was almost permanently green as we mowed the strip for the station.

Plane with Flowers & Storm

Conferences

Every two years, Frontier Services hold a three-day Patrol Ministers' Conference. Whilst we were in the patrol, it was always held in July, in Alice Springs. We attended the 1984 conference, even though we did not start in the patrol until January 1985. The conferences were great times of fellowship.

For the 1986 conference, we flew our little plane from Meekatharra to Warburton Range, where we refuelled before flying on to Alice Springs. In future years, we flew to Uluru and then onto Alice Springs, which meant a six-hour flight without a toilet stop for the first leg of our journey, so we would have nothing to drink after four o' clock the day before we flew to Uluru. One year, when we landed in Alice Springs, there was a very large USA Globemaster waiting for us to land and taxi past him before he could take off. We felt very small passing him. The conferences were a wonderful time of fun, laughter, friendship, recharging our batteries, and spiritually uplifting ourselves with worship, services, and great speakers.

Soon after, I drove the Frontier Services car on to Kalgoorlie, for an Isolated Parents Children's Conference, taking one of the visiting Frontier Services staff with me, while the other stayed with Bob to work on the Women's Health Issues in our area.

We had planned to stay for two nights in Kalgoorlie, so that we would be driving back in daylight after the conference. However, on the day of the conference the weather forecast was for strong showers on the unsealed road between Kalgoorlie and Sandstone. I knew that this particular road closed even with a very small amount of rain. As it was important that we were able to get back to Meeka, I reluctantly decided to drive to Sandstone—even though I knew part of the trip would be after dark. About 70 kilometres from Sandstone, an old man kangaroo leapt straight in front of me, hitting the roo bar. He pushed it back to almost touching the engine, damaging the front of the vehicle, although it was still drivable. We carried a spade in the back to dispatch any badly hurt animals, if needed. The roo had been injured, but bounded away. Although concerned about him there was no way I felt safe looking for him in the dark in the bush. My only hope was that he was not badly injured. Even though there did not seem to be a great deal of damage, the cost was $1,500. Less than the cost of the damage to the plane!

The Pilots' Strike
In 1989, during the pilots' strike, Meekatharra's uncontrolled airfield became very busy. Instead of the usual daily Sky West plane, we had numerous small charter planes calling in to refuel. On one day there were five of us waiting to take off, while two incoming planes were wanting to land. This put a lot of strain on patience and airmanship. We all got away in the end, and there was no compromise on safety.

Later on in the strike, I wanted to go to the Solomon Islands to be with my daughter when she had her fourth baby. I drove to Perth, caught a flight to Adelaide, before flying on to Brisbane a week later, which was the next available flight, before finally flying onwards to the Solomon Islands. In the end, my beautiful new grandson arrived before I did!

Problems
In the summer of 1990 we had some interruptions in our flying, although fortunately nothing major. The first problem was with the directional gyro, which failed on three separate occasions. The directional gyro is the instrument which is used

to maintain course. It is much more stable and far easier to use than the compass, but the problems with the directional gyro meant that we became much more adept at using the compass for navigating. Then, on one trip, the compass sprang a leak and became much less reliable. Bob managed to stop the leak before all the fluid was lost, and we kept on flying.

The second hiccup came when the nose strut went flat. Bob had been told of a bush repair for the condition, and spent the day fitting a rubber hose sleeve on the shock strut to replace the effect of the oil and air pressure. It worked well.

Finally, we had a magneto failure before take off. Although life in Meekatharra often required unconventional solutions to everyday problems, on this occasion we had to abandon flying until we could get a replacement—and an engineer to fit it. This took three days.

CHAPTER 26
After Meekatharra: Jenny

Sandstone Centenary

We were invited back to Sandstone after we had retired at the end of 1993. The Sandstone Centenary was held in 1995, as part of the centenary celebrations of finding gold in the area.

Sandstone has grown since we left, with a grand total of eighty-nine people in the 2016 census, but at that time of the centenary celebrations there were 40 people living in the town, which of course also supported the surrounding stations. The community had received a grant for the celebrations, and they hosted an incredible weekend. Bob was asked to arrange a church service on the Sunday, alongside the Catholic bishop and the Anglican minister from Mount Magnet.

Sandstone Post Office

In their planning, the centenary committee anticipated about 600 people would attend the celebrations. In the end, about 1,100 people came for the weekend. In their preparations they had planted a lawn at the campsite, and kept it watered, which was a very large effort. They had also spent the previous year putting together a museum showing the history of the community. However, of even greater significance was what happened to the old Catholic church.

When the bishop heard about the centenary, he donated the Catholic church to the town, to be used as a non-denominational church. The town received another grant of $10,000 to repair the church. The repairs and renovations included painting the interior and exterior of the building, taking out the confessional and the high altar, and replacing the old louvre windows, which used to let in a great deal of red dust. The new windows are clear glass, with an edging of stained glass. Finally, the highlight of the renovations was a magnificent stained glass window, depicting Christ pouring out billy tea to gathered people, surrounded by animals and birds. The wall in which the window is set faces west, so it is stunning to see on a sunny afternoon. Christ could be a bronzed Aussie, an Arab or an Aboriginal—it is a magnificent work of art. They had planned to clean and polish the floor, but ran out of time and money for that.

The Programme

Friday Evening

We arrived on the Friday afternoon and settled into the accommodation that had been arranged for us. The evening was very relaxed, with people finding friends they hadn't seen for a long time and sitting around, with a small band wandering amongst the tables and chairs, singing country-and-western songs.

Saturday
The day started with a parade and a book launch. It was very hard to have a parade with such a small community, although a number of station people were there as well as townsfolk. Even so, it had been arranged for the Geraldton City Band to come over for the weekend, and for a number of vintage cars to come up for the parade. The last 120 kilometres of the 600 kilometre journey from Geraldton was over dirt road. The parade was headed by the eight Sandstone schoolchildren, one of whom square gated, and then a float with the CWA group dressed in old-time clothes. The fire brigade and representatives of the nursing post and RFDS followed the CWA, then came the band and the vintage cars, and finally the people from the stations.

The book launch followed after the parade, to mark the publication of an excellent book on the history of Sandstone.

The events of the morning were followed in the afternoon with the opening of the museum. We were amused when two nuns, whom we had not met during our time with the patrol as they had only moved to the area after we retired, rushed over and greeted us very warmly, calling out to the bishop that we had arrived.

In the evening it had been decided to hold a dinner dance. As there was no building in which such a thing could be held, and with an anticipated 600 people in attendance, a shade cloth had been erected around the tennis courts. The Geraldton City

Band played again for the dinner dance. A problem arose when it became apparent that there were going to be many more than 600 people. As it was not possible to host the full 1,100 visitors for the dinner dance, silent movies were shown for those who could not fit in for the dinner dance.

Sunday

The dinner dance finished at around 2 am. As the church was far too small to hold the number of people expected for the service, all the chairs that had been hired for the dinner dance were set up outside the church. Bob had organised with the bishop and the Anglican minister as to who would do what for the service.

Bob arranged for the bishop to start and to finish the service, with Bob preaching, and the Anglican minister reading a passage of scripture and saying a prayer he had written for Mount Magnet Centenary the year before. All went well, and at the end the bishop asked if he could tell a joke.

The Joke

An itinerant priest was visiting a town similar to Sandstone, when a little boy rushed up with some newborn kittens, proudly telling the priest, 'They are good Catholic kittens, Father.'

'Bless you, my boy,' replied the priest.

The following week, the priest returned to the small town. The same boy rushed up, with the same kittens, proudly telling the priest, 'They are good Protestant kittens, Father.'

'Now wait a minute,' said the priest. 'Last week, you told me they were good Catholic kittens!'

'Oh yes,' said the boy, 'but now they have their eyes open.'

Sunday Afternoon
The Sunday afternoon was fairly free, with a demonstration by the fire brigade and a burial of the remains of a man, a miner, who had been killed in a mining accident nearly 80 years before. They had recently reopened the mine as on open cut, and as the approximate position of where the man's remains were known, they were very careful digging up that section. They found his remains, and it was decided to have his burial during the centenary weekend. They knew his name, but not if he had any faith, and so it was decided that the bishop would carry out the service, in case the man had been Catholic. One of the people attending the service was an elderly man who had been a very young child when the accident at the mine had happened, but he was too young to have known the man who had died. At the end of the service, the bishop told another joke.

The Second Joke
There was a man who died and went to heaven, to be met at the pearly gates by St Peter.

'You may go wherever you wish,' said St Peter. He pointed at a few different groups of people, explaining, 'The Anglicans are over there, the Presbyterians are over there, and the Lutherans are over there.'

'What about the Catholics?' the man asked.

'Oh,' St Peter replied, 'They are behind that brick wall over there, because they think they're the only ones here.'

The Messiah

The last part of the weekend was a performance of The Messiah, which was held a couple of kilometres out of town at a lovely breakaway. The committee had arranged for seating for about 600 people, so the announcement was made to bring a folding chair or a rug if you had not booked. The breakaway had the name of London Bridge, as one end had worn away to resemble a bridge.

We were sitting right up high at the back, and with a choir of just thirty people I thought we may not hear everything, but fortunately we heard every word. It had been arranged for volunteers from the Western Australia Symphony Orchestra, along with a number of retired members and a few people from the Western Australia Youth Orchestra to stay at a station on Saturday night, along with with the choir and four soloists.

Many people there had never heard such music. In fact, I was sitting next to a young man who had obviously had his arm twisted to come for the evening. It was an incredible rendition of The Messiah. Three of the soloists were astounding, and the fourth was very good. At the interval I asked the young man sitting next to me what he thought of it. He was absolutely awe-struck and thrilled, telling me that he had never heard anything like it. So often people in the bush do not get any live performances of any sort.

Yalgoo

Three other times whilst in the patrol we had visits from members of the Western Australia Symphony Orchestra. On one occasion, the members of the Chamber Orchestra and the

WA Symphony Orchestra came up to Yalgoo to play before going on to Geraldton the following evening. One of the members looked in the tin shed they were to play in and saw a few men standing around with their tinnies. He said, 'You'd better take some of those chairs away, it's not good playing to empty chairs.'

'It's all right, mate,' the men replied.

That evening, all 140 chairs were filled, with extra chairs having to be brought in. They stopped for an interval with a very good supper and at the end of the concert there was a singsong around the piano until four in the morning!

We heard later that when they went to Geraldton they had an audience of 30 people, so they were happy to come back again to the Murchison, which they duly did for the bicentenary celebrations, when a ball was held in a beautiful old stone shearing shed, all spruced up for the occasion. Most of the WA Symphony Orchestra played all night.

Golden Wedding

The year 2004 saw our Golden Wedding Anniversary. Bob had wanted to wear a wedding ring for some time, and this seemed like a great opportunity. He wrote new vows for us and we renewed our commitment to each other in our church. Bob's best man came over from Melbourne with his wife. My matron of honour was not well enough to come over, so my eldest daughter Mandi took her place. Our son Ian read a lesson, and our daughter Fiona sang. It was a pity that our youngest daughter, Ailsa, could not make it over, but in spite of that, it was a wonderful occasion with a good party to follow.

Golden Wedding Anniversary

South Korea

In 2011 we were invited to join Australian veterans of the Korean War on a visit to South Korea, as guests of the Korean government. It was an extraordinary time, both exciting and humbling. We were driven around by bus, with 'War Veterans' emblazoned on the side. Everywhere we went in the bus, the people we passed—even the youngest children—bowed, and the Korean war veterans saluted. When we met Koreans at events they would always thank Bob for the sacrifice he made. At one banquet a general heard that Bob and I had been engaged to be married whilst Bob was in Korea. The general turned to me and thanked me for my sacrifice.

Two years' later, Bob was invited back to South Korea with fifty-nine others, to celebrate sixty years since the signing of the truce. One of the highlights was when a girl read a poem that she had written, and then she and her little sister gave each man a national flower. The veterans also went to Busan, in the South, where the overseas troops had first joined the war, with the troops from Ethiopia being the first to arrive. Busan is where the war graves cemetery is located. Bob and another friend located the grave of Bob's best friend in the RAAF, who had been killed shortly after they arrived in Korea.

Our OAMs
Much to my surprise, in October 2010, I received a letter from the Governor General of Australia offering me the Medal of the Order of Australia (OAM), for community services, including Girl Guiding, the Embroiders Guild of SA, and the Country Women's Association. The award was to be announced on the 26th January 2011, should I choose to accept it. The condition of acceptance was that no one was to be told about the award before the 26th January 2011.

I could not believe what was happening! I made an exception to the condition of acceptance and told Bob, knowing he would keep it secret. I then replied to the Governor General accepting the award by return mail. Four months was a long time to keep the secret.

The Investiture was not until the 13th of April. One of our granddaughters had come over from WA with her small daughter. Technically, we were only allowed two guests each, but Bob, Amy, and Eva were able to come, as Eva was deemed too small to count.

The day dawned clear and bright, we were all dressed, up, out to the car, early as usual. Unfortunately, we had a flat battery, as one of the car doors had not been fully shut after taking the pram out of the car the night before. We rang the RAA and explained the situation, and they said they would be there as soon as possible.

As I had to be there before the others I started to get worried and decided to catch the bus, as it only took ten minutes to get into town. The bus delivered me safely into the city, and I hurried across to Government House, still on time. The others arrived shortly afterwards, which put my mind at rest. Bob was very pleased for me, and I was very glad that he already had the Air Force Cross (AFC).

Our excitement happened all over again a few years later, when Bob received a similar letter from the Governor General in early 2015. It was a secret time again—this time we had to wait almost six months for the announcement to be made on the 8th June 2015, which was the holiday for the Queen's Birthday. What a thrill! Bob's award was also for service to the community, particularly through Church and Veterans organisations.

This time, the Investiture—on the 27th August 2015—went smoothly, and our son attended with Bob and me.

The Sydney Harbour Bridge Climb

In 2016 we were visiting our daughter Fiona and her family in Sydney, and decided to climb the Sydney Harbour Bridge. I was not sure Bob would want to climb it, but they assured us that we would not be right on the edge and we would be tied onto the bridge, so there would be no problems.

Sydney Harbour Bridge Climb

When we arrived they very thoroughly checked to see if we were fit enough for the climb.

"We don't want to call a helicopter in to take you off the top of the bridge," they explained.

"Not unless I'm flying it," Bob muttered in reply.

We went through the hoops with no problem, but when I mentioned I was in my early eighties this threw the climb leader into a fit. So we didn't bother telling him that Bob was six years older.

It was perfect weather for the climb, and we had wonderful views.

Blue Sapphire Anniversary

In 2019, we flew to Canada and took a wonderful trip, starting in the Rockies, taking the train from Lake Louise Vancouver, and then on a ship up the coast.

One of the highlights of the holiday was a lovely helicopter trip. The weather was perfect and the colours of autumn added to the magic of the flight.

We travelled on to Jasper where we celebrated our anniversary with cakes, chocolates, a small bottle of Champagne, and a ride on a Harley Davidson—as pillion and sidecar passengers.

Bob's Passing

We had to put Bob into Mary Potter Palliative Care very unexpectedly on the 24th July 2019. He wanted to go into care, and not die at home. They were wonderful to both him and all the family. We had been told it would only be a few days when he went in as he had severe jaundice. Somehow he battled the jaundice and it calmed down. Time went on with many of the family able to get over and see him, including Amy from Perth and Fiona from Sweden, where she was visiting her son and his wife.

As time went on the doctors and I were surprised that although not able to get out of bed and obviously getting less and less well, he was still able to converse and go on with life.

On the 2nd September, on my birthday, Bob and I celebrated, along with our son Ian and his wife Jane. The staff brought a cake, and we all raised a glass. By that stage, Bob could only have whiskey brushed on his lips.

The following day, still with no pain, Bob slipped away

quietly and calmly. Amy told us afterwards that he had confided in her that he planned to hold on until after my birthday.

He had a wonderful celebration of his life on the 9th September at Christ Church UCA, with 200 people present, and many more watching on the live stream from around Australia and from overseas. The Air Force took the role of pallbearers, with a bugler playing the 'Last Post' and 'Reveille'. An Air Vice Marshall read part of the *Eulogy*, and a piper piped him out of the church at the end of the service. Bob would have been overwhelmed, and would have thought it all a lot of fuss.

I have been so supported by people over the last two years, with people saying how much they miss him, and how much they loved him.

As a family, we think he was a very special person.

www.ingramcontent.com/pod-product-compliance
Lightning Source LLC
LaVergne TN
LVHW051558070426
835507LV00021B/2646